What people are saying about
TEAM CLEAN
& CAROL PAUL

• •

"There is no I in teamwork. Everybody knows that. But nobody wants to clean up the house, either. So Carol Paul has brilliantly solved the problem of making responsibility fun again! She approaches the job like a big league sport. And she may also have found the glue that brings every family together."

– Brandon Parker
The Washington Post

"What a great idea to u͟r͟   , busy, overworked, stressed out mom. The l͟.   ͟.ɪ this are infinite and the fact that you get a clean h   ͟.ɪeless. A win/win for parents and children!"

– Tina Gä. ͟.eri Head Cheerleading Coach – Baltimore Ravens

"I've been part of some great teams in my life, DeMatha High School, Harvard University, *The NFL Today*, and *Inside the NFL*. There is a lot to be learned from being a team member. This book shows you how to take the team concept and use it with the most important people in your life—your family. I can't think of a greater way to invest your time!"

– James Brown "JB" Sportscaster
The NFL Today, **CBS /** *Inside the NFL*, **Showtime**

"Having a 'game plan' is essential for a successful team. I was motivated to get my family team back on track, and having *Team Clean* as a playbook was inspiring, easy to follow, and motivating. My family was excited to have a goal to work toward together, and our first month on the program has a been a huge win for our family."

– Lura Fleece Cheerleading Coach
University of Maryland – Head (1992–2007) Asst. (2007–present)

"The most important team you'll ever coach is your family, and this book will show you just how to do it. It's a must read for a busy parent trying to make sure to keep family time in the schedule."

– Mike Krzyzewski "Coach K" Head Basketball Coach – Duke University
Basketball Hall of Fame class of 2001

"Carol Paul is organized to a fault, but you will love her and wish some of her would rub off on you! She has turned a mundane chore into a well-oiled event. She has broken the parts down so it can fit any household."

– Silvia Hill Owner – Professional Organizing Systems – A & H Movers

"I have lived my life with the priorities of God, Family, School, Basketball. After reading this book, I am thinking I might amend them to: God, Family, School, TEAM CLEAN!"

– Morgan Wootten Coach Emeritus, DeMatha Catholic High School
Basketball Hall of Fame class of 2000

"Every mother is really a head coach. In this book, Carol Paul breaks down all the tasks involved in keeping house, as if cleaning is football camp. Tasks are plays; kids and parents are players; disorder and mess are the opponents. Voila! Your family is once again a team. And they live in a spic-and-span home."

– Meg Daly Olmert Author of
Made for Each Other—The Biology of the Human Animal Bond

"As a coach, I can tell you that kids thrive from being a part of a team. Put this concept into action and the life lessons your children will get out of it are countless. Some things are better taught through the coach/player method, and this book gives you a way to do just that!"

– Mike Brey Head Basketball Coach – Notre Dame

"*Team Clean* is a "must-read" book that is jammed packed with priceless information to make house cleaning a fun sport the whole family can play.

-Susan Friedmann, International Best-Selling Author of
Riches in Niches: How to Make it BIG in a small market

"Magician, Therapist, Scientist…I am not sure what she is…but Carol Paul has done it! She will have your family asking you if they can clean each week! A truly family spirited book…a must read for every parent."

– Patrick Snow International Best-Selling Author of
Creating Your Own Destiny **and** *The Affluent Entrepreneur*

"A close family, life lessons for your children, and a CLEAN HOUSE—what more could you want? This quick read can make it happen overnight!"

— **Geraldine Valentino-Smith State Delegate – Maryland**

"*Team Clean* is a testament to the value of family activities. Not only will Mom get a cleaner house, but Dad will bond with his children, and children will grow up being responsible, secure, and ready to take on life as adults."

— **Tyler R. Tichelaar, Ph.D. and author of the award-winning *Narrow Lives***

"I met Carol Paul while volunteering for a 'FUNDAY' Spring Fair when our children were attending the same grade school. Under Carol's leadership, this little school fair was transformed into a powerhouse fundraiser year after year. She could coordinate a setup/breakdown crew that could compete with any concert-tour crew in the music business. She's amazing!"

— **Jim Hossick Songwriter / Performer – ChildrensMusic.com**

"Carol Paul is the perfect combo of: motivator, event planner, and positive energy. Her Team Clean concept promises to strengthen your family bond while building discipline in your children. A book worth reading!"

— **Doug Peters State Senator – Maryland**

"Carol Paul shouldn't be a housewife/mother! She should be coaching the Redskins. Except coaching the Skins is way easier! The world has been waiting for this book. So has the floor underneath the sofa."

— **Dr. Michael Olmert Professor / Emmy award winner**

● ●

"I really feel sorry for people that go through life and never know what it was to be a member of a team."

– Rob Breedlove
All-Pro Linebacker
Washington Redskins

● ●

THE END OF CLEANING ALONE

TEAM CLEAN

The Ultimate Family Clean-Up-The-House Formula

CAROL PAUL

AVIVA
PUBLISHING
New York

Published by:

Aviva Publishing

Lake Placid, NY

518-523-1320

www.avivapubs.com

ISBN: 978-1-938686-50-4

Library of Congress 2013906860

Editor: Tyler Tichelaar

Cover Design: Meg Dentler

Cartoonist: Kevin Stamper

Interior Design: Fusion Creative Works, www.fusioncw.com

First Edition

For additional copies visit: www.TheTeamClean.com

Also available as an ebook

There is no greater feeling than being part of a team. And your family's about to get that feeling!

This book is dedicated to my team:

· ·

Steve, my husband, the leader of our Team
And the best "players" ever
Stephen, Bucky, Kiersten & Charlie

And to my mascot:
The late Loretta Capitello Wilson
My best friend and "partner in crime" for
thirty-six years

Ellen Degeneres…
I want to be on your show
…so we can dance!

Special Thanks To Those Who Made Team Clean Happen

• •

To my nephew, Nick Stamper, who was the most excited about me writing *Team Clean*. He constantly asked me how it was coming along and refused to let me give up on the idea. He believed in its success when nobody else did. Nick, I often say you are the reason this book came to be!

To my cousin, Betsy Greaney, for being the first "outsider" to read the book and for being one of the first families to try our Team Clean system.

To Silvia Hill for being an early witness to our family's Team Clean and adding her feedback.

To my brother-in-law, Mike Stamper, for all his advice and time concerning the legal aspects of writing a book!

To my sister, Tricia, for her help with publishing, copyrights, patents, and more. You were the first to tell me I was an author. You taught me so much!

To Dr. Michael Olmert, for taking the time to read my first draft and give me personal feedback. He is second to none when it comes to mentors. I will forever be grateful for his time, advice, and positive response!

To the professionals who made this book actually "hit the shelves." I couldn't have asked for more time or personal attention, and I can't imagine how anyone could possibly publish a book without each of the amazing people on my publishing team: Kevin Stamper, Meg Dentler, Shiloh Schroeder, Jessi Carpenter, Tyler Tichelaar, Susan Friedman, and Patrick Snow. They are a first class operation!

To my sister, Cathy, for always patiently listening, offering suggestions, reading my drafts, and trying out Team Clean from the beginning days with her own family. Thanks for letting our days at the gym, on the treadmill, be all about "my book"! You have always been there for me no matter what. You are a true friend!

To my parents, Morgan & Kathy, for being such great parents and giving me the foundation to love being a parent myself. You showed me that traditions are an integral part of what makes up a family. Thanks to my dad for "rubbing" off on me in so many ways. Priorities, priorities, priorities! Thanks for being such a great "teaching" parent! Thanks to my mom, for showing me what I really wanted to be in life at such a young age. I always knew that when I "grew up," I wanted to be a "mom" because you made it look like the best job in the world! I wanted to be *you*! Thanks for being such a patient, loving parent who always had time for me. I will always be in awe of your strength and humility.

To Stephen, Bucky, Kiersten, and Charlie for letting *Team Clean* be the main subject of conversation in our home during the writing of this book and always offering feedback and support when I talked about it. You never stopped showing interest in this endeavor or teaching me how to do things to get it done, like saving the book when my laptop "crashed"! People say you can't be your children's friends, but I am not so sure I agree. I truly enjoy the time I spend with each of you! People often ask what stage of childhood I like best, and I always say, "Whatever stage my children are in!" You are all so good to me. Time with you fills my soul. Thanks most of all for writing your chapters from the heart. Reading them was a true joy for me!

To my husband, Steve, for his advice, encouragement, and numerous reading and re-reading of chapters, but most importantly, for helping to establish Team Clean in our family; for that, I am so thankful. You have always supported whatever project I indulge in and given me your full support. Since the day we met, my happiness has mattered to you, and you have always wanted me to "be me," and for that I feel so blessed!

Contents

● ●

Foreword by Morgan Wootten	21
Introduction	25
Team Clean Building Blocks	31
A Little History	35
Chapter 1: Team Clean is Born in Our Home	39
Chapter 2: Decluttering the Playing Field	45
Chapter 3: Acquiring the Right Game Equipment	59
Chapter 4: Learning the Fundamentals of the Cleaning Game	67
Chapter 5: Preparing the Weekly Game Plan—The Chart	81
Chapter 6: Establishing Jobs and Playing Positions	87
Chapter 7: Including Visitors—Fans	101
Chapter 8: Moving Beyond Housework—Creating a Family Tradition	109
Chapter 9: Establishing the Coach	121
Chapter 10: Coaching the Team—Getting the Family Team to Work	125
Chapter 11: Keeping Up—Quarterly Cleaning Jobs	135
Chapter 12: Taking It on the Road	143
Chapter 13: Convincing Dad to Get Involved	147
Chapter 14: Hearing What Our Four Kids Have to Say	153
Chapter 15: Learning Lessons from Team Clean	169
Chapter 16: Checking In on Life After Team Clean	173
Chapter 17: Commenting on Your Comments	179
Chapter 18: Prepping for the Weekly Team Clean	187
Chapter 19: Laying the Foundation for Team Clean	193
A Final Note	199
Take Note...	202
Appendix I: Chart Samples	207
Appendix II: Job Samples	215
About the Author	222
I Can Coach You on How to Coach Your Team!	224
Carol Paul will come speak to your group...	226
Coach Wootten's Basketball Camp	228

Foreword

· ·

When I first began to coach at St. Joe's Orphanage, I quickly learned it took teamwork to get anything worthwhile done. I realized early on it was amazing what could be accomplished if no one cared who got the credit. This is the whole concept of a team; when the participants will park their egos at the door and desire to be part of something greater than themselves.

When my wife, Kathy, and I settled in and started to raise our family, we found that teamwork could almost become contagious. From the early days, we found that giving our children responsibilities was a real key to their becoming confident, hardworking kids. As a coach, I found that most often the great players came from hard working, organized families.

I always referred to my teams as the "DeMatha Family," and all the fellow coaches I knew used the term "family" to talk about their players and teams. Carol has taken this concept and reversed it to refer to families as teams! In this book, you will learn all about her Team Clean system. You will see how she has created a way for children to reap the benefits of playing for a team just by being a part of their own Team Clean family. The rewards and lessons kids can get from Team Clean remind me of the same values I saw our players learn over the years. The benefits of learning those values are endless.

When you follow the formula and strategies that Carol outlines, you will find that you have created a special night in every week of the year that your family really looks forward to. It is said that the best family interaction happens at mealtime, but after observing Team Clean, I have witnessed regular family bonding like no other.

Something I found special is to see a youngster start off knowing only one skill and then slowly learn each and every skill until he or she becomes the whole package. In basketball terminology, we call that the complete player!

In *Team Clean*, you will learn that only by working together can great things be accomplished. There is no letter "I" in team, and there is no greater feeling than a team realizing it has done its best to become the best it is capable of becoming. You can give your family the gift of feeling this feeling! Carol will show you the way! She has taken the entire idea of teamwork and shown everyone how to make team cleaning a real adventure. I have always told my players to play hard, play smart, play together, and have fun. With Team Clean, your kids can do all four of these things!

Most of the greatest accomplishments in life are done through teamwork. It took a team to put a man on the moon. It will take a team to make your house sparkle. Giving your children the opportunity to become members of a team is one of the greatest gifts you can give them.

Morgan Wootten
Basketball Hall of Fame 2000
Coach Emeritus, DeMatha Catholic High School

Introduction

● ●

You do all that you can just to get your family through the day. You use your weekends just to catch up. You do just enough laundry so people have clothes to wear; you are constantly cleaning the kitchen, making sure it is ready for the next meal to be made; you pick up toys and clutter so everyone can safely walk through the house (or at least so they aren't in eyesight of the unexpected visitor!); you make sure the trash is taken out when it's full; you hope all your family members' items can be found before they walk out the front door each day, and you try to get a new roll of toilet paper in the bathroom before the last one is empty, all the while hoping nobody stops by at the wrong time, especially your mom! And for some reason, nobody in the family is jumping up to help!

Maybe you have decided to pay someone to clean for you. Maybe you buy convenience food and pre-packaged items. You have tried to streamline. You are playing the role of coordinator. No matter how good you get, somehow it is still up to you to find everyone's missing belongings or to make sure everyone has a clean towel when he or she gets out of the shower! No matter how hard you try, the family days are just slipping by with everyone rushing in and out, trying to make sure everyone's schedule or deadline is met. And in the meantime, it is eating away at the family budget.

The cost of having someone else clean your home once a week averages $7,800 per year, not to mention the money it costs to replace items that you know you have, but you just can't seem to find. With that extra $10,000 per year, you could go on a pretty nice shopping spree!

● ●

"If you have two children, three years apart, and they move out when they are eighteen years old, and you run Team Clean instead of paying for weekly cleanings, you could save $210,000 in those twenty-one years of raising the two of them!"

– Steve

"Co-founder of Team Clean"

● ●

Are you and your spouse working full-time jobs? Are you home alone with the kids all day? Are you driving all day and barely have a moment at home? Are your children not pulling their weight when it comes to chores? Do you have to ask your kids over and over again to do something? Are you doing way more than half of the household chores? Do you have to beg for help? Is "family time" defined as driving to and from school, games, and practices? Do you consider your children interacting with each other when they sit side-by-side watching TV, texting, playing a video game, or going through the drive-thru line at your local fast food place? Is your intimate relationship with your spouse limited to waving to each other as you pull in and out of the driveway? Was this the family you dreamed of when you got married and first had kids? Do you want to stop playing "catch up" and start enjoying your family and your home?

I get it! It is very hard when you feel like keeping up the house and building a great family at the same time are all up to you. I understand how overwhelmed you feel. I know how underappreciated a mom can be at times. I know how you wish there were more hours, more days, more hands. I know how it feels always to feel behind. I know because I have four children of my own.

Team Clean will walk you through the process of turning your family into a team that cleans together once a week. You will learn how to prepare your home for Team Clean and what few items you need to make it work. I will show you how to get your family on board, and I will help you figure out what role each member will play, depending on his or her age, gender, and abilities. I will teach you how to break the jobs in your house down to simple three-part directions and show you step-by-step how to run the actual cleaning night, with advice about avoiding obstacles. You will learn how to cover cleaning your entire house in less than an hour, without cleaning any other night of the week.

There is a Part II to Team Clean that turns this weekly "clean up the house night" into a family bonding night, and this book will teach you how to make that happen in your home too. We will brainstorm together and build the perfect Part II for your family. You will learn how to establish and implement it on your very first Team Clean night. (Your family will love this part!) I will show you how this tradition will benefit your children for life, strengthen all the relationships within your family, and even build bonds with your children's friends. This last part really comes in handy when they become teenagers. You will even get a chance to hear the dad's and kids' points of view, but in the end, you may be most excited to learn that you'll never clean your house alone again!

I have raised four children and I established Team Clean in our house twelve years ago in the fall of 2000. My children ranged in age from four to thirteen when we did our first Team Clean. I co-own an overnight basketball camp where we instruct 2,500 kids every summer. I organize the rooming (by request!), teaming, registration, and check-out each week. I chair numerous community non-profit events throughout the year. I started a youth group from the ground up. I have always coached my kids' teams and led their afterschool activities. I have run playgroups for toddlers and overnight weekends for teenagers. I know how to implement systems and create ways for things to work efficiently! I make sure whatever I am doing is run the best way possible for the least amount of time and money.

You might think that I don't understand where you are or that your family members are different than mine. This is not true. I was in your shoes. Our children never even had chores before Team Clean. The closest we ever got to making our children work was singing the Barney "Clean-Up" song as we had them put their toys in the toy box!

I want to share the Team Clean concept with you. I will teach you how to be the coach of your family by being your coach! I will lock arms with you and show you how I went from my children not having chores, to my family *asking* to help me every week.

●●●●●●●●●●●●●●●●●●●●●●●●●●●●●●●●

*"I can honestly say I look forward to doing Team
Clean every week."*
– Bucky
our son – started Team Clean at age 10

●●●●●●●●●●●●●●●●●●●●●●●●●●●●●●

I will show you how cleaning can be a mere "blip" in your week. It takes twenty-one days to form a habit. I say, in ninety days, you can create a solid tradition that will produce lifelong benefits for your loved ones. What is the date of ninety days from now? Write it down. It will be a good day for you and your family.

Today is the first day of your ninety days. You are about to learn the Team Clean system. When you look back to this day, it will be like looking back at the "before picture" in one of those diet books. You are making a decision to take the step to rebuild and strengthen your family, and as an added bonus, you will get a clean, organized house, and your very own team will be the one making it happen for you! I know I can help you achieve this transformation for your family. Let's take this journey together.

Are you ready to start? Give me a "T"! Give me an "E"! Give me an "A"! Give me an "M"!

Let's create your team!

Carol Paul

· ·

"We made Team Clean a condition of our grown children living at home. We thought for sure it was too late and that our parenting was done, but we have had tremendous success. It's never too late to start!"
– Paul & Annie
"Friends of Team Clean"

· ·

Team Clean
Building Blocks

"Coming together is a beginning. Keeping together is progress.
Working together is success."
– Henry Ford

Team Clean will teach your family how to do all three things in the above quote. I will lead you step-by-step through the whole process. It will be quick and painless! You will learn to implement this system in your family in no time at all, and to help you through it, I have created what I call "Team Clean Building Blocks."

Throughout this book, you will find the Team Clean Building Blocks. These blocks are meant to help you build your Family's Team Clean. They are hints about what I have seen work (and not work) in our family and in other families' weekly Team Clean rituals.

As you read, highlight the Building Blocks pertinent to you. Take note of them in the "Take Note" section. Write them down and post them on your fridge. Make this book your workbook. You will be glad you did. It will become an invaluable reference once you implement Team Clean in your home.

The Building Blocks are meant to get you thinking. Maybe add your own notes to a block to make it fit your family members or let it spur a thought that you want to put in your personal "Take Note" section. The more you jot down now, the better prepared you will be for your family's first Team Clean night.

After you start your Team Clean, the Building Blocks are what you will most often refer to when making your family *come together, keep together, and work together* on your road to success!

A Little History

• •

"Those who do not learn from history are doomed to repeat it."
–George Santayana

• • •

In 2000, I would have said my husband Steve, our four kids, and I were middle of the road people when it came to cleaning. We were definitely not obsessive (in fact, not anywhere close!), yet we didn't live in filth (maybe chaos, but not filth).

We taught our kids to help, but we never gave them job assignments or specific duties like dinner dishes. We used more of an "individual ask for help" method. After dinner, I might ask one of them to clear a dish or two. If I brought clean clothes into their rooms, I might say, "Hey, can you put these away in the right drawers?" In the fall, my husband would have the kids help rake the leaves. They never had a task that they called their own or a duty they knew they were responsible for. At this point, we had never taught them that someone was counting on them for something.

As for how we kept the house clean…well, I guess we just did what we needed to do to get through the day. I did what laundry needed to be done, picked up clutter and toys the best I could, took the trash out when it was full, and cleaned up after meals; that was about it.

Every time we wanted to have people over for dinner or even just to hang out and play cards or a board game or have drinks, it was a crazy, mad rush to clean the entire house. Steve and I had to take on every room in the house and all in a matter of a few hours! We first had to find a place to put all the clutter, and then after that was done, we had to go back and clean it!

Steve loves to cook and I love to entertain, so we found ourselves in this hectic situation quite often. The sad part was, we had to rush through the part we loved—the cooking, decorating, and setting up—because we had to put our energy into cleaning.

I loved to set out candles, build an inviting table, and create the perfect atmosphere for a wonderful party. Steve loved to pick out great food and even concoct a special themed cocktail. We always got it done. We pulled it off without a hitch and the house looked "picture perfect." Our "secret" was safe, but I am not sure it was the best way to be doing it, for us or for the kids.

The whole day leading up to when we would entertain that evening, I would find myself annoyed if the kids took a toy out or wanted to do anything that might mess up my progress. The nerve of them wanting to play on their day off! This was how we spent many weekends. We became quite good at it since we entertained a lot.

Twelve years later, we are still middle
of the road people when it comes to
cleaning (not obsessive, not living in
filth), but the chaos part is gone. We
still love to entertain (often!), but we no
longer spend our weekends cleaning and
we never clean before company
comes over.
(Not one thing!)
We enjoy the fun of getting the party
ready instead. Our children spend time
with us on the weekends but not a
moment of it is on housework.
We have discovered a concept that we
call Team Clean, and it has changed our
lives in "oh, so many ways!"

Team Clean is Born in Our Home

● ●

"People don't like having to do tasks by themselves—especially housework. Rather than doing chores separately, it can be a much more positive experience when families do them at the same time."
– Barbara Schneider

● ● ●

The youngest of our four children is an August baby so his birthday normally falls when we are on vacation at the beach. For the first three years of his life, his parties were quite simple…all the cousins on the beach with water balloons, popsicles, and glow sticks. The year he turned four, his birthday fell on the day we were heading home, so he asked whether everyone could come to our "real" house for a big party. I was a wreck. I knew how I had left our real house when we had headed out on vacation two weeks earlier! Panicking, I called a cleaning service long distance and told them where to find the hidden key and hired them to clean. I mean…my MOM was going to be there…I had to do something!

We arrived home to an immaculate house and the party was wonderful! After everyone left, I thought about what I had done and felt ridiculous that I had paid someone to bring a team of people into my home to clean it when I had my very own team that lived there. I realized the cleaning service had probably been in the house for about an hour…and I thought "My family can spend one hour together doing what that service did…and I won't have to write a check in the end!" So I told my husband and he jumped on board immediately.

He took my idea to a whole new level with a detailed plan on how to pull it off. His Team Clean plan did so much more than give us a permanently clean house. He gave us a weekly family bonding night and a tool to teach our children every cleaning job there is to keeping up a house. Through Team Clean, he taught our children responsibility and commitment. He taught our children obligation, rules, priorities, and a sense of duty. This sounds crazy, but Team Clean, in some ways, was our biggest form of discipline. It was rare that we ever punished or restricted our children.

TEAM CLEAN

They say the key to discipline is that if you threaten, you have to follow through with the threat. I used to imagine a whole crowd of people watching me after I would threaten the kids. The imaginary crowd was there to see whether I was going to follow through. It helped put the pressure on to make sure I carried out the "punishment." Team Clean is a little like that. You have told your kids it is something they have to do, and you have to follow through. It isn't a big deal, but it teaches them you have expectations for them that they can't get out of. This sets a great tone for how your house runs.

We believe we have created a gift that, hopefully, our children will bring to their future families, which will make not only their families, but their marriages stronger.

●●●●●●●●●●●●●●●●●●●●●●●●●●●●●●●●

"I am not sure when I first bought into the whole
thing, or any of my siblings for that matter,
but now doing Team Clean once a week just seems
like second nature."
-Bucky
our son – started Team Clean at age 10

●●●●●●●●●●●●●●●●●●●●●●●●●●●●●●●

Team Clean has been tremendously successful in our house. (And in so many more ways than just keeping our house clean!) We want to share the concept with other families and households. This short book will walk you through the process of getting started, motivating reluctant kids and spouses, and forming your own family Team Clean tradition. Odds are, you are either currently cleaning your house alone, paying hard-earned money to have someone else do it, or have given up on cleaning all together. By following this simple plan, you can transform this dreaded chore into a fun family event that will bring about results you never would have imagined.

. . . .

"Team Clean all started because my parents did not like to spend money. They were frugal, or as I like to call it, cheap. My parents thought it was crazy to order a maid service when the whole family could pitch in and clean the house just as well."

-Kiersten

our daughter – started Team Clean at age 8

. . . .

Decluttering the Playing Field

. . . .

"Clean up…the maid is coming today."
– Anyone who has ever hired a maid

• • •

We all know that most people joke about cleaning up for a maid to come. I have even heard people say, "I had to stop getting my cleaning service; it was just too much work getting ready for them." The truth is, pre-cleaning for the cleaning crew is step one of cleaning. I like to call it decluttering. If you do it correctly, it is not something you have to do each week. When we first started Team Clean in 2000, we took on a major decluttering project. I went to the library and checked out books and really tried to do it right. It paid off too. It is so much easier to clean when you have less to clean around.

My favorite of all the books was Alice Fulton-Osborne and Pauline Hatch's *It's Here Somewhere*. I even checked it out months later for my friend, trying to get her on board. When the library called to tell me it was overdue, I called my friend to get it back and she couldn't find it. As she searched her house, she said, "I swear it's here some-where…" At that point, I realized she obviously hadn't used the book! So find the book or system that's right for you. Find what motivates you. But the more items you move out of your house, and the more items you assign an exact place for, the better your Team Clean will be.

We decluttered one space at a time. We made a list of every space in the house. Every space on our list counted as a place that needed to be decluttered. So we began with room number one. We took everything out of the space and started with a blank canvas. I think this is a very important step. Make sure you move it all out! Don't just go through things. You will get tired halfway through and just move things back in place. You will be tempted not to go through everything. If you move it all out, you actually have to decide to keep something and put it back. If it stays out for a few days until you finish, that's okay. This is your project right now. Think of it like painting a room. It's a mess for a while, but it will really look good in the end.

TEAM CLEAN

Some rooms have many "spaces" within them. List every space that needs to be decluttered, not just rooms. Treat each space as a separate place to declutter.

We sorted all the items into six categories:

Keep in this space

Keep in another place in the house

Storage/memory item

Giveaway

Return to owner

Trash

Keep in this space: If it made it to this pile, it had to have a specific place to go. We were very careful when putting items back in place. We made sure they had a very specific place in the room/space. We bought containers and boxes, hung hooks and shelves, and labeled places. Items that might have been kept in more than one place in the past—for example, Scotch tape, batteries, and other small stuff—could only have one place in our new system. Since 2000, we have never had a junk drawer. If we decided to keep something, it had to have a place in our house! You might be thinking we must be organized or obsessive-compulsive, but that is far from the truth! You would not think our house is any different from anyone else's if you walked into it. The big difference is that we don't have extra stuff, and we tend to know where most things are. We tend to get rid of things more easily since this major decluttering overhaul.

Keep in another place in the house: If we had already determined a place for the items in this pile, then at the end of this space's overhaul, we re-stocked them to their correct location. Items that did not yet have a determined place were saved in the garage until they fit a category. If they were things that belonged in a room or place that had not been decluttered yet, we would put it in the "yet to be decluttered" room to be sorted at its proper time.

Storage/memory: Everyone in the household was allowed one memory box. Each person got to pick out a special box. Some just chose a Rubbermaid one in his or her favorite color; some chose a cute basket. I have an old hat box of my husband's grandmother's. Each person's box is in the top of his or her closet, and he or she is allowed to keep as many memory items as will fit in the box. For papers, each person has a binder and we three hole punch any papers that he or she wants to save and keep them in there. We have dividers in them labeled with each school year.

TEAM CLEAN

When deciding whether to keep my kids' papers, I ask myself, "Would I want this if my parents had kept it for me?" This has helped a lot!

Giveaway: We bagged up giveaway items immediately and tied them tight. We didn't want anyone changing his or her mind. I took the giveaways to our local Goodwill once a week.

TEAM CLEAN

Many societies will pick your items up right from your front door and even leave a tax receipt for you!

Return to owner: We created a "lost and found" area and made a point to return items to people who had left things at our house.

I still have a designated shelf in our basement that holds our lost and found items. The kids' friends are always leaving items behind, so it is nice to have a place where even those items belong! Of course, now that it's snowboards, surfboards, coolers, and bikes, the shelf seems to be a little small!

Trash: (my husband's and my favorite pile). This whole pile goes right to the can and out to the curb!

Our motto during the decluttering process was:
Make a place for everything we want to keep—
if it doesn't have a place, we can't keep it.
This meant two things:

- We only kept what we had to

- We had to be creative about where to keep it

Everyone keeps food in cabinets and clothes in dressers, but here are some of the more creative spaces we came up with:

- We got rid of all extra sets of sheets. Everyone kept his or her one favorite set. This meant we did not need to store sheets anywhere, and it also meant no folding sheets ever again! Each week when we wash sheets, we just put them right back on the bed.

- We got rid of all of our extra towels. Everyone kept a favorite towel and kept it on a hook in his or her room. This meant we did not need to store towels anywhere, and it also meant no folding towels ever again! Each week when we wash towels, we just put them right back on the hooks in everyone's room. We did put a dresser in our upstairs hallway to hold our beach towels and a few extra bath towels for guests.

- We gave each of our kids a "spot." The spots were in random places in our house. One was a corner. One was a chair. One was a crate, and one was a basket. This was each one's spot to keep things that didn't go to his or her room. They could put their backpacks there or their sports items or books they were reading or something they needed for the next day. These spots were also great places for me to put any items of theirs that I would find around the house. I even used the spots as a place to put things I needed to "deliver" to my family members, like signed permission slips, school forms, milk money, mail, a handwritten reminder note—you name it. Having this spot for each of them really solved so many issues. It was rare that an item couldn't be found for school or practice because it was always in the person's spot. After a few years, my kids' cousins would come stay with us for a few days, and without fail, they would demand that we make a spot for them too!

- We turned our foyer coat closet into our cleaning closet. My husband put some shelves in it, and it houses everything we need for Team Clean. It's where we keep all our cleaning supplies, lightbulbs, batteries, keys, flashlights, a bucket of rags, and our rug vacuum.

- In each full bathroom under the sink, we have a supply bucket. It holds rags, glass cleaner, cleaner w/bleach, soap scum remover, and a magic eraser. There is no transporting of cleaners each week on Team Clean night. They are right where you need them.

- We turned our linen closet into a supply closet once we got rid of all of our towels and sheets. We have a category on each shelf. Toilet paper on the top shelf. Oral supplies on the next shelf. First aid on the third shelf. Shower supplies on the fourth shelf. Hand soap and lotion on the bottom shelf. We added shelves to the inside of the door for medicine bottles.

- We keep the leaves to our dining tables under our bed so I decided why not keep what goes with them there too! We purchased an under-the-bed box and store all our formal tablecloths and table linens in it. Different cloths that I use to decorate the table go in there too. When it comes time to get the table ready, everything is all in one place.

- We share hats and gloves and mostly wear them when it snows. So it made sense to me that they are all stored together rather than in each person's room. We made one of the family room end tables into a square trunk, and it houses all the scarves, hats, gloves, ear bands, etc. This method has not only worked well for us but also for friends who come over to go sledding!

- We cleared off our bathroom vanities and tried to hang as much as possible. We even installed hooks and shelves and containers on the inside of the cabinet doors to hold make-up, toothbrushes, razors, hairspray, etc. We tried to pick a place for everything we used. We knew that if everything were hanging and up off the counter, cleaning would be a breeze!

- We put a wastebasket in every room. My husband and I disagree on this issue. He thinks that the following trash cans are all you need: one in each bathroom, one in the kitchen, one in the basement, and one in the laundry room. I say, one in each room. I think it is more realistic that a kid will throw something away if it is easy to do. My husband says that the trash job is cut in half on Team Clean night if there are less cans to empty, but I say, trash that doesn't make it to a can, and in turn has to be picked up, would generate more work than the time it takes to empty a few more wastebaskets on Team Clean night. So as you can see from line one, we decided to go with the basket in every room. Think it through and decide what works best for you!

- We cleared off all the counters in the kitchen, just like the bathroom. We tried to put back only what we had to. We hung the toaster oven. We hung the coffeemaker. We hung the electric can opener. Left on the counter was our blender that we use twice a day and our fruit basket. We also have a holder for paper plates, cups, and napkins.

- I found a cute five-drawer dresser (on the side of the road!) and brought it home. It fit perfectly in our kitchen, and we immediately named it the homework drawer. It houses pens, pencils, loose-leaf paper, folders, book report covers, graph paper, calculators, rulers, colored paper, maps, dictionaries, and everything our kids ever needed for homework.

One of our four kids has a harder time than his siblings at getting rid of things. He thinks he should hold on to a sixth grade science paper and he is twenty-two years old! When we declutter with him, we have to have a few more piles. He needs the standard six above, plus three more. The first is *give to my brother or cousin*. He feels better if someone in the family has the item he is not quite ready to give up. I guess he finds comfort in the fact that he could always ask for it back. The second category we add is *store for a certain reason*. He keeps some items for summertime at the lake, or if he ever plays paintball again, or if he goes to the Maryland game, and the list goes on. We box these items and label them for the event/occasion. The last category we add for him is *keep in the attic in case I want it later*. This category helps him put off the decision of giving something away. Now remember, he has a memory box, so if it is really important, it would be in there. If his attic pile is not asked for after a while, I know what I can and can't get rid of. He is incredible and enjoys numerous activities, so he does have more items than the normal person. He has four bikes! Needless to say, he needs a few more spots than the rest of us around the house, so he has a few cabinets in the garage for the stuff he needs to get to on a more daily basis.

This complete decluttering and reorganizing project is obviously something that cannot be accomplished in an hour or two. It will take some thought, time, and effort over multiple days. (If I remember correctly, mine took over a month!) But it is a crucial first step to making Team Clean successful.

TAKE NOTE...

Make a list of all the rooms in your house

Example #1	Example #2
Room: Master Bedroom	Room: Bathroom
Spaces to declutter in this room: Closet Mom's Dresser Dad's dresser Under the bed Amoire Mom's nightstand Dad's nightstand	Spaces to declutter in this room: Under sink Linen closet

Now you make your lists. (Make them for every SPOT in your house!)

Room:	Room:
Spaces to declutter in this room:	Spaces to declutter in this room:

Room:	Room:
Spaces to declutter in this room:	Spaces to declutter in this room:
Room:	Room:
Spaces to declutter in this room:	Spaces to declutter in this room:
Room:	Room:
Spaces to declutter in this room:	Spaces to declutter in this room:

Room:	Room:
Spaces to declutter in this room:	Spaces to declutter in this room:
Room:	Room:
Spaces to declutter in this room:	Spaces to declutter in this room:
Room:	Room:
Spaces to declutter in this room:	Spaces to declutter in this room:

Room:	Room:
Spaces to declutter in this room:	Spaces to declutter in this room:
Room:	Room:
Spaces to declutter in this room:	Spaces to declutter in this room:
Room:	Room:
Spaces to declutter in this room:	Spaces to declutter in this room:

Acquiring the Right Game Equipment

··

"Some say opportunity knocks only once, that is not true.
Opportunity knocks all the time but you have to be ready for it.
If the chance comes, you must have the equipment
to take advantage of it."
– Louis L'Amour

● ● ●

I am a part owner of an overnight basketball camp. One weekend, I was in the dorms after the campers had checked out when I saw the cleaning crew come in. They had swept all the food, candy wrappers, and other kid-generated trash out into the main hallway. I was amazed at the amount. Then I saw them run a commercial vacuum through the hall and suck it all up! I thought, "I need one of those at home." When we started Team Clean, I remembered back to that day, so I made a call to the housekeeping department and found out the make and model of the vacuum and ordered one immediately. It cost me $189.00 and has lasted twelve years.

A good vacuum not only makes the carpets look better, but it also extends the life of the carpet by getting more of the grit up. Commercial vacuums may be a little heavier than household vacuums, but their performance, durability, and cost more than make up for the little extra weight.

For our floor vacuum, we use a shop vacuum, which is a wet/dry vac that we have set to the dry function. We use an eight gallon one. We have had the same one since day one of Team Clean. These wet/dry vacs have incredible suction power since they are designed to suck up large quantities of water. Dry dirt and dust is no challenge for them, and they can also vacuum up larger items such as a bowl of spilled peanuts or even broken glass. Also, they are incredibly light and easy to carry around the house and up and down the steps. Choosing this vacuum as your floor vac allows you to assign vacuuming the floors to a pretty young child.

We think it is important to use two separate vacuums for floors and rugs. First of all, you are able to get the vacuum that is best for each surface, and secondly, two people can be working at the same time. We keep a twenty-five-foot extension cord on each vacuum. This means less unplugging as you vacuum. It is probably smart to figure out the length you need to do the largest level of your home and get that size. Our second son has always been in charge of vacuuming the rugs and is famous for yelling, "Unplug me!" when he is ready to move on to the next level of our house. The extension cord means we have to run to unplug him less often! We keep extra bags for the shop vacuum and extra belts for the rug vacuum in our cleaning closet at all times.

We do not use paper towels at all. We have been married twenty-five years, and the only time I have ever bought paper towels is for our annual crabfeast each June! We have an old five-gallon paint bucket full of rags. You can buy your rags, or you can use old washcloths or dishtowels. You can even go buy a few old towels at the local thrift store and cut them up. We keep a second basket of rags under the master bathroom sink. We use rags to clean everything, with the exception of the bathtubs and showers. I use Mr. Clean Magic Erasers for them.

You will always need to have trash bags in stock. You need trash bags for every size trash can—your kitchen trash can, your room wastebaskets, and your recycling (brown paper bags possibly). I think you should have a wastebasket in every room of your house.

As far as chemicals go, we only use five cleaners. They are all in spray bottles.

Window cleaner

Cleaner with bleach

Soap scum remover

De-greaser

Furniture polish

When we started Team Clean, we turned our entry level coat closet into a cleaning supply closet. My husband put four shelves on the closet's side wall and left the middle open for the vacuum. A well-stocked cleaning closet makes Team Clean run smoothly each week. It also means kids know where to find their supplies and, just as importantly, where to put them away.

This is what we keep in there:

- Rug vacuum

- Hand-held rug steamer/cleaner

- Bucket of rags

- 5 spray cleaners (I usually have 4-5 of each of these so we never run out)

- Lightbulbs (every type used in our house)

- Batteries

- Book *How to Clean Practically Anything* by Consumer Reports

- Extra vacuum cleaner bags and filters

- Extra vacuum cleaner belts

- Vacuum attachments

- Window squeegee

- Extension pole for squeegee

- Brush for cleaning lint from under fridge

- Brass polish

- Silver polish

- Car cleaners

- Rug shampoo

- Knee pads (to wear when cleaning a hard floor)

- Two fly swatters

- Chair pads

- Wood floor cleaner

- Wood floor refinisher

- Bug spray

- Ant traps

- Toilet bowl bleach tablets

- Keys (for some reason I keep all spare keys in this closet!)

- Suction cups (We decided on this spot for them during our declutter process years ago!)

- Flashlights

Normally, if we start to run low on an item, my husband will mention it to me. Whenever I restock items (especially the five main spray cleaners), I buy at least 6-8 bottles, or better yet, the large refill bottle, which generally is a little cheaper.

Besides the cleaning closet, we have a cleaning supply bucket under the sink in each full bathroom. In it we keep three spray bottles (glass cleaner, cleaner w/bleach, and soap scum remover), Mr. Clean Magic Erasers, and rags. We keep a toilet brush to the side of each toilet in our house. We keep our kitchen trash bags under the kitchen sink and our wastebasket bags under our master bathroom sink so they are closer to where the wastebaskets are.

We have two storage places for our shop vac. We created the two storage spots so no time is ever wasted. One is on the top floor of

our house and one is on the bottom floor. This way, you start vacuuming on the floor you finished on the week before.

Don't forget the uniform. Everyone must have Team Clean clothes.
Just like you wear paint clothes to paint, you should wear Team
Clean clothes to clean! Our Team Clean clothes now have bleach
spots all over them. We feel awful when a guest joins us for Team
Clean and we forget to tell him to put on Team Clean clothes and
he ends up with a bleach spot. Our kids have a specific place in
their closets where they keep their Team Clean clothes. (Of course,
these can also double as their paint clothes.)

A team must have a good equipment manager! Be
prepared by having everything you need for each
cleaning job. That way there are no excuses not to
clean something that week.

Learning the Fundamentals of the Cleaning Game

• • •

When you open a new item you have just brought home from the store, it normally comes with instructions for how to put it together or make it work. The ones that come with less than five step-by-step instructions make it seem so easy that almost anybody could do it. Team Clean is no different. It's a new concept you are bringing home. We have broken each job in our house into simple step-by-step instructions. When you read them, you might start to think that cleaning really isn't that hard. You will definitely think it isn't worth your hard-earned money to pay someone else to do it!

My dad and brother are both coaches, and they have always told me that they would rather get a player who doesn't know a skill at all than a player who has been doing the skill wrong for years. It is so hard to change a bad habit. It is always better to learn to do something the right way and then practice it correctly until it becomes second nature. In the early days of Team Clean, it is worth your time to show each person how to do his or her job the correct way. Teach it in these easy simple steps. Personally, I rush through my jobs. Cleaning fast does not mean you are not doing a good job. If your kids (and spouse) want to do their jobs fast, there is nothing wrong with that.

When my second son was in grade school, he couldn't learn through reading. (Funny that he ended up becoming an English major in college!) When the teachers would assign homework that required reading something and then answering questions at the end, he skipped the reading part and would just circle random answers. He would go to school the next day, get credit for doing the homework, and "learn" everything as the class went over the answers. He then knew the information and did fine on the test. I was horrified when I realized what he was doing. I went to school and told on him! The people I met with told me they were actually impressed that he had found a system that worked for him. They tried to tell me that he was actually pretty smart to find a way to compensate for his weakness. They pointed out that he didn't just try to get out of the work but rather, he developed a system that worked for him so he was able to achieve the same desired end result: learning the material. I wasn't too convinced and never really agreed, but I can relate it to Team Clean now. If one of your team members has his or her own way of getting the job done and it seems "too easy" or "fast" for you, or maybe it is in a different order than you would do it, back off. As long as the job is done in the end, people have a right to go about it in the way that fits their own personalities. One of the great things about Team Clean is that when you look around, cleaning the house does start to look a lot easier than you had thought it was all those years!

* *

"The best way to do Team Clean is just to get it over with. There is nothing better than finishing early and watching everyone else struggle through their jobs."
-Charlie
our son – started Team Clean at age 4

* *

THE BATHROOMS

My husband put himself through college as a lead janitor at an all girls' high school. He learned quickly how to clean disgusting bathrooms efficiently. You will be surprised that we don't use any paper towels and not much water. It really doesn't take long to clean a bathroom, much less a whole house!

FULL BATHROOM:

Step 1

- Spray the mirror with glass cleaner.

- Spray the sink and faucets with cleaner w/bleach.

- Wipe the mirror dry.

- Wipe the sink and faucets dry (and clean).

- Splash water on the faucets after you wipe them and wipe again—see the shine!

Step 2

- Spray the ENTIRE toilet (seat, lid, back, sides, bottom near floor, inside, etc.) with cleaner w/bleach.

- Spray the shower/tub (and shower curtain/doors) with soap scum remover.

- Wipe clean the entire outside of the toilet.

- Clean the inside with the toilet brush.

Step 3

- Wet the magic eraser and wipe down the walls and floor of the shower.

- Let sit while you take all rags to the laundry room floor.

Step 4

- Come back to wet the magic eraser again, and use it one more time to finish the shower.

- Rinse with water.

DONE!

HALF BATHROOM:

We like to call this chore sink/toilet/mirror because that's all the job is!

Step 1

- Spray the mirror with glass cleaner.

- Spray the sink and faucets with cleaner w/bleach.

- Wipe the mirror dry.

- Wipe the sink and faucets dry (and clean).

- Splash water on the faucets after you wipe them and wipe again—see the shine!

Step 2

- Spray the ENTIRE toilet (seat, lid, back, sides, bottom near floor, inside, etc.) with cleaner w/bleach.

- Wipe clean the entire outside of the toilet.

- Clean the inside with the toilet brush.

(Notice that you don't use much water!)

Cleaning the bathrooms was a job I always hated before Team Clean, so I was pretty bummed when it was assigned to me when we started this weekly ritual. However, doing this chore with my team each week has totally changed the job. I no longer empty the trash, pick up the towels, vacuum the floor, or clean the floor. It's like the job has been cut in half. Best of all, now when I am done cleaning the bathrooms, I walk downstairs and the whole house is clean!

VACUUMING

Our second son has always been in charge of vacuuming the rugs. He started at age ten. His job is to vacuum every rug surface in the whole house, including the two sets of stairs. He has never missed a Team Clean. He puts on his iPod, plugs in the vacuum, and gets to work. He now attends college and lives on campus, yet he rides his bike home (twenty miles) every week to do Team Clean (and eat with us!).

RUG VACUUM:

- Vacuum all rug surfaces (well!).

- Make sure to get every inch of them.

- Rugs include stairs, if they are carpeted.

My niece is the youngest of five children. When she was four, I went to her house to teach her family how to do Team Clean. I gave her the job of the wood stairs. She used a hand-held duster and dusted each step down to the bottom. In the end, her older brother came by and vacuumed up the pile at the bottom. The stairs looked great and she *loved* doing the job! This method is a creative way to "vacuum" stairs that are not carpeted and to include a younger child in Team Clean.

· ·

"I have probably vacuumed more square feet of rugs in my life than anyone my age."
-Bucky
our son– started Team Clean at age 10

· ·

FLOOR VACUUM:

- Vacuum all hard surface floors (well!).

- Make sure to get every inch of them.

- This includes stairs. Carpeted or not, the shop vac should be used on the edges.

● ●

"All I had to do was put my headphones on
and the floors would be done before I knew it."
-Kiersten
our daughter – started Team Clean at age 8

● ●

CLEANING THE FLOORS

When my youngest son was six or so, he would do any job that involved a spray bottle. We came up with the idea that he could do the bathroom floors, and then the person doing the bathrooms would start to think cleaning bathrooms was easy once floors were not part of the job. The bonus was that a bathroom floor didn't gross him out.

BATHROOM & LAUNDRY ROOM FLOORS:

- Spray floors with cleaner w/bleach and wipe dry. (remember someone has already vacuumed them!)

- Replace clean bath rugs.

DONE!

● ●

"I remember one of my roommates saying she didn't
know how to clean, and I was SHOCKED."
-Kiersten
our daughter – started Team Clean at age 8

● ●

TRASH/RECYCLING

Our trash person normally tucks extra bags in the waist of his pants and grabs the kitchen trash can and heads upstairs to dump all the little wastebaskets into it. Since he has extra bags right with him, it makes it easier to replace bags in any cans that need it. Our Team Clean falls the night before trash day. We have always made taking the trash all the way to the curb part of the job. Normally, my husband makes the recycle/trash person sing Jack Johnson's "Reduce, Reuse, Recycle." Like I said, it's the little things that turn Team Clean into a family tradition with memories!

RECYCLING:

- Put newspapers and magazines in brown paper bags.
- Place filled bags where recycling goes in your garage.

DONE!

TRASH:

- Take one large trash bag or trash can around the house to every wastebasket.
- Empty contents from each wastebasket into large bag/can.
- Replace cans with new bags when necessary.
- Take trash all the way to the CURB!

DONE!

THE KITCHEN

I *love* to make popcorn. I use an old pot and put oil in the bottom and then the kernels. I put it on the stove and wait for it all to pop, giving it a shake every so often. Once it's done, I douse it with Old Bay Seasoning and YUM! Well, my husband's Team Clean job is the kitchen, and without fail, he always starts with my dirty popcorn pot! The poor guy would probably love it if just once that pot was clean and put away. But, hey, like I said, Team Clean is all about repetition and tradition. I am just making sure I keep the weekly ritual intact!

I recommend having Dad do the kitchen. Normally, Mom spends a lot of time in the kitchen on a daily basis, so if she has to do it on Team Clean, it just feels like "one more time" that she has to clean the counters!

KITCHEN:

Step 1: The Table

- *The "Wood" Table*

- Clean it with a damp rag.

- Dry it with a hand towel.

- Spray it with furniture polish.

- Buff it with a clean dry rag. (This is the only time I will mention elbow grease—put some power behind your buffing!)

The "Nonporous" Table

- Spray with bleach cleaner.

- Wait a couple of minutes.

- Wipe it off.

Step 2: The Microwave Oven and Stove

- Take removable parts and put them in the sink.

- Spray degreaser on all surfaces (including the removable parts you just put in the sink—lift the stove if you can; get underneath; get everywhere!).

- Wipe off with a damp rag.

- Dry the surfaces with a hand towel until they are residue free and shiny!

**If you have a toaster oven, it should be cleaned the same way as part of this step.

Step 3: Counters

- Clear *all* items from the counter. (I usually place these items on the newly cleaned table.)

- Spray the counters with bleach cleaner (or recommended cleaner for your counter type).

- Wait a few minutes.

- Wipe off with a damp rag.

- Dry the counters with a hand towel. (This insures that no residue is left behind and that they have a nice shine.)

Step 4: The Sink

- Spray the entire sink surface with bleach cleaner, including the fixtures.

- Wait a good five minutes for the bleach to kill all the germs.

- Then rinse well.

- Dry the fixtures with a hand towel to ensure a shine.

Step 5: Vertical Surfaces

(Includes the exterior of the refrigerator, dishwasher, cabinets, etc. Do as needed.)

- Make a quick check for spills or other spots.

- Spray and wipe.

Step 6: The Floor

(Wait until the floor vac person has finished vacuuming the kitchen to do this step.)

- Check for spots.

- Spray with bleach cleaner and wipe.

The kitchen chairs used to be a job all in itself. When our kids were younger and messier, the chairs held great clues about what we had eaten for our last few meals. Now that the kids are older, and all food goes into their mouths, we really only have to do the table.

KITCHEN CHAIRS:

- Get a hot damp rag.

- Wipe down and scrub chairs.

- Rinse rag with *hot* water if necessary.

- Dry chairs.

DONE!

ADD ONS

After a few years of enjoying our clean house, I added the washer/dryer job to the list. I was doing laundry one day when I thought it would be so nice if the machines were always dust free. Adding that job to the Team Clean list was a pretty easy way to make sure they would be.

WASHER/DRYER:

- Spray washer.

- Spray dryer.

- Wipe the washer dry (and clean).

- Wipe the dryer dry (and clean).

DONE!

● ●

"If it wasn't for Team Clean,
I wouldn't have the faintest clue how to
clean a house."

-Charlie

our son– started Team Clean at age 4

● ●

Preparing the Weekly Game Plan—The Chart

"Nothing great was ever accomplished without enthusiasm."
– Ralph Waldo Emerson

• • •

The chart is the weekly Team Clean plan. It's worthwhile to print it out each week to give all participants a written plan of action to follow. Even when everyone has his or her job memorized, the chart still serves its purpose of organizing and tracking progress.

My family has been doing Team Clean for twelve years and we still print the chart each week. We put it on the kitchen counter before Team Clean starts. If we have a visitor, his name goes on the chart and he gets job assignments. My only rule over the years has been that visitors can never do bathrooms! If we have a special job to add for the week, like take down the Christmas wreath or sweep up the spilled dirt on the patio, we add it. But for the most part, the chart stays the same each week.

We name our Team Clean each week, just for fun. It is the first line of our chart. We name it after people's birthdays, we name it after good report cards, and we name it after big events like championship games and awards received. We name it after holidays, our church events, world events, and even after small funny things. My husband came up with this idea. I never realized at the time that all the little things he added when we created Team Clean were what made it work so well. These small touches are what turned a weekly cleaning into a special event—a solid tradition and not just housework.

The top half of the chart lists the person's name and his or her job assignments. Our children always have their individual bedrooms listed as one of their jobs. They are expected to have their floor clear enough for a vacuum and their clean clothes pile put away. (That's it.) They normally do these tasks once they get their Team Clean clothes on.

The center of the chart is for the whole reward of Team Clean! Each week, we order takeout for dinner once Team Clean is complete. We rotate who gets to choose where we order from. We, as the parents, have set the budget. We try to keep it at $30-$40 for a family of six. Be clever…ordering Outback kids meals can be very affordable. Keep coupons! So, on the chart's line one, we write who the "orderer" is. We started with our oldest child the first week we ever did Team Clean, and then we went in age order. Occasionally when one of our children can't decide what he or she is in the mood for, that child will trade the honor of being the orderer with a sibling, in exchange for that sibling's future night. The "orderer" writes the name of the restaurant he or she wants to order from that week on the designated line of the chart (labeled "restaurant"). When team members check their job assignments, they check which restaurant has been chosen and write in their specific meal orders in the space at the bottom of the chart. This activity creates a positive feeling right away as the team members check their chore lists. Instead of just thinking about the jobs they have to do, they are thinking about the great meals they just ordered!

Next to the chart, we always put out a highlighter. As people complete jobs, they highlight them. Checking off a completed job tracks progress and gives the worker a sense of accomplishment. It is amazing how the job feels more complete when you can see it highlighted or crossed off on paper. And working off the chart can actually be a subtle way to teach the kids to work from a list of things to do. This is a simple but valuable life skill.

Below is our family's Team Clean chart:

Team Clean: _Charlie made the honor roll!_

Jobs

Bucky	Vacuum Rugs	Vacuum Steps	Bedroom		
Kiersten	Vacuum Middle Level Wood Floor	Vacuum Basement Floor & Hall	Pick Up Dinner	Bedroom	
Charlie	Clean Laundry Room Floor	Clean Bath & Laundry Floors	Refill Toilet Paper	Bedroom	
Carol	Lake Bathroom	Beach Bathroom	Christmas Bathroom	Crab Bathroom	Wash All Towels Rugs & Sheets
Steve	Kitchen Table, Micro-wave, Stove	Toaster Oven, Can Opener, Clean/ Shine Sink	Water Plants, Dust, Change Light Bulbs	Bleach Counters	
Stephen	Trash & Recycling	Make Two Beds w/ Clean Sheets	Bedroom		

Orderer: _Stephen_

Restaurant: _Chipotle_

	Order
Bucky	steak bowl – black beans, rice, corn, hot salsa, gvac, cheese (extra) plus chips
Kiersten	chicken bowl – rice, veggies, tom, corn, sour cream, gvac, cheese
Charlie	Steak bowl– black beans, rice, veggies, tom, corn, hot salsa, sour cream, gvac, cheese, lettuce plus chips!
Carol	1/2 chicken – 1/2 steak salad, veggies (extra), mild salsa, gvac, lettuce
Steve	Carnitas tacos – pinto beans, rice, veggies, hot salsa, cheese, lettuce
Stephen	chicken burrito – both beans, rice, mild salsa, hot salsa, gvac, cheese, lettuce

Establishing Jobs and Playing Positions

• •

"Let everyone sweep in front of his own door, and the whole world will be clean."

– Johann Wolfgang von Goethe

• • •

Have you ever had someone ask you to do a few things and you were so good at it that the person added more for you to do? I grew up in a family of five children, and my youngest brother jokes that every time he came home, there was a list of things for him to do. I guess the other four of us had moved out and the work was all on him. He claims that whenever he completed items on the list, my parents would just write a few more things on it. To this day, he has nightmares about the never-ending "To Do" list. When he was first married, his new wife made a short list for him. I am pretty sure it was just for him to go to the grocery store, but she said she had never seen him so adamant about *not* wanting her to do something ever again! Team Clean should only be *one* night and not take too long. Do not start to pile on jobs because it is working so well. Take the time now and decide from the beginning what jobs need to be done. Making this list upfront is a very important step. It will be okay to add small items later, but try to include the bulk of your needs from the beginning. The beauty of Team Clean (and the big selling point to your family) is that it is a one-time gig that lasts less than an hour! It can't become the "never-ending" Team Clean or the family will rebel.

TEAM CLEAN

I prep for Team Clean each week like I would for a maid service. I quickly declutter by getting everything to its correct place, and then I strip two beds and grab towels off hooks. I wash all the towels, bath rugs, master bedroom sheets, and just one of the kids' rooms' sheets. This means the kids' sheets get done every third week. I start all this wash the morning of Team Clean. During Team Clean, I keep the wash going and make the two beds and put the towels back on their hooks.

The very first time you introduce Team Clean, it is best to start with the whole house. This is very important. It may seem tough or overwhelming at first, but kids will "buck the system" if you add jobs later. It's better for them to know their workload from the beginning and take ownership of it. After a while, they will actually start to think of their jobs as manageable as their assignments start to become secondhand to them. The sooner you can determine each person's permanent job, the better off you are.

● ●

"I have never switched jobs doing Team Clean."
-Bucky
our son– started Team Clean at age 10

● ●

It is very tempting to add jobs to a child's list when he finishes early. If a child finishes early, he has earned the joy of being done. DO NOT ADD a job. When he finishes what you listed on the chart for him, he is done!

Try to think about what things you have to do once a week and make a list. You can include anything. We just acquired a new coffee maker that has to be cleaned out once a week in order to run properly (what a pain). Well, guess what just went on our Team Clean list!

TEAM CLEAN

Our youngest has a weekly assignment for school where he has to call his German teacher and leave a message in German. He never remembers to do it. We decided to add it to his Team Clean list, hoping to teach him to work from a "To Do" list to keep up with his assignments. There are all kinds of things you can add to Team Clean!

Here are some examples of weekly items to include:

- Change lightbulbs (most weeks none will need to be changed)

- Change sheets

- Change towels

- Water plants

- Sweep the front porch/back patio

- Refill toilet paper

- Fill hand soap dispensers (most weeks they don't need refilling!)

- Throw out magazines/newspapers

- Pet-related jobs

Next, think about what you need to clean in the following two places and write it down:

KITCHEN:

- Stove

- Counters

- Microwave

- Table/chairs

- Sink

- Appliances

BATHROOM:

- Toilet

- Sinks

- Mirrors

- Showers/tubs

- Floors

Finally, think about items that need to be addressed throughout the entire house and write them down:

- Rugs

- Floors

- Empty trash

- Dust

Try your best to include all the jobs on day one of your Team Clean. If you add jobs later, your family will buck the system.

Now it is time to divide the jobs into even parts according to the number of people on your team. Think of it as being like picking out presents for the holidays. You might buy some bigger ones and some smaller ones, some cheaper ones and some more expensive ones, but in the end, you try to make each person's "pile" equal. Sort the jobs into the number of "piles" you need for your household and play around with what jobs should go into which pile until you feel the piles are equal. Once you have divvied up the jobs, try to assign who might be the best match for each assignment. Think about things like who might like the same job throughout the house instead of switching what he is doing, who might like multiple jobs and different jobs, who is better at putting supplies away and can handle a job with more supplies, and who might be grossed out by some jobs. We even had to think about allergies. Our oldest can't handle the chemicals like the others, so bathrooms can never be on his list. You should think about who might be better at certain jobs than others. Take strength and ability into consideration. In the beginning weeks, or even months, of Team Clean, assignments can be on a rotating basis until you figure out who should be doing what. It may take some rearranging of jobs to get people in the right "position" and also to get the exact right jobs together in the right piles. Take note of who is good at what, who likes what, whose jobs might just be too much, and which jobs go best together. Our youngest was four when we started Team Clean. Young kids can do this!

• •

"If you wanted an easy job (like me),
then that meant you had to do more of them."
-Kiersten
our daughter – started Team Clean at age 8

• •

My neighbor once told me that when it comes to your own children, the prime working age is ten to thirteen. He said that before ten, children want to help so badly, but it's more work on the parent to let them help than just to do it yourself; from ten to thirteen, they are still willing and finally old enough to be of help, and after age thirteen, they are able to help, but for the most part, they are unwilling. Jump on the willingness of the pre-ten year old! Assign a two year old the job of putting all the toys in the toy closet or putting the trash in the trash can. Assign a three year old to hold the dustpan or dust the stair edges. Assign a four year old to sort the clean silverware from the dishwasher or to carry all the old magazines or newspapers to the recycling bin. Assign a five year old to spray and wipe the bathroom floors. Assign a six year old to carry all the clean clothes piles to the right locations. All young kids can vacuum, especially with a light shop vac. My neighbor did have it right; it is more work on the parent in the beginning, but we have learned that it is well worth it in the end!

Remember, they will not be too young for long. And, in the meantime, they will be glad to be working with the rest of the family. From the very beginning, they will think of themselves as part of the team. When they are ready, it will be easy to move them on to "real" jobs. When our second son was two years old, he had a toy lawn mower. When my husband would go out to mow the grass, Bucky, without fail, would go out with his toy mower and follow him around. Bucky knew he was helping to mow the lawn and he felt grown up. We jumped on this and always made sure to call Bucky when it was "time to cut the grass." As our kids have grown up, Bucky has always been the one to volunteer to mow the lawn. Somehow, it became his job in his mind from an early age, and he doesn't even remember the toy lawn mower. It is amazing what two and three year olds can learn from watching and imitating parents and older siblings. So if your three year old wants to follow you around the house with a dust rag, not only should you let him, but tell him it's his job. It may seem like he is in the way and slowing you down, and he may be, but he is also learning to be part of Team Clean. You may even want to buy your little ones a toy vacuum cleaner. Whatever it takes, toy, real needed job, or made up one, make sure your kids have assignments on Team Clean night as soon as you can.

Everyone who lives in the house should have jobs, even if you have to make up unnecessary ones!

Once you have determined the "final" assignments for your family, there will still be days that Team Clean doesn't go smoothly. Two bumps along the road that we found were:

Some kids, not all, always tend to think that another person's jobs are easier. It's just ingrained in their personalities. We found that trading jobs a few times will either prove to them that this is not true, or you may get lucky and they will find the perfect jobs for themselves as they try the other ones out.

When a child just does not cooperate or doesn't do his/her job well, we choose to remove him/her from the cycle of being the "orderer" for one full rotation.

● ●

"I always thought someone else's job was easier or better than mine. My family likes to tease me about this, often."
-Kiersten
our daughter – started Team Clean at age 8

● ●

Your kids will not fall in love with Team Clean overnight. Some will take much longer than others to accept the weekly ritual. Before Team Clean, we occasionally hired cleaning services. My two middle kids would be so upset after the cleaning people would come. My son would complain that they had moved all of his stuff. It would make him so mad. My daughter was convinced stuff was missing because things were out of place. How spoiled! Well, in the early days of Team Clean, I remember them coming to me and begging to get the cleaning people back. They promised they would never complain about them again. I think my son even told me he had made it all up and nothing had ever been moved. They wanted out of Team Clean, and they would have said anything to make it happen. Unfortunately for them, we knew we were on to something good; there was no way we were turning back!

Stick it out. Even if you do this at 50 percent, it's more that what you were doing!

And news to me after reading my kids' chapters…

• •

"We would also trade jobs between the kids.
If one kid hated one job and the other hated
something else, they might trade jobs up. If the two
jobs weren't quite equal work, then you would have
to trade multiple things. Once we even did a three
person trade."
-Charlie
our son – started Team Clean at age 4

• •

Boy, could I go on and on about what lessons can be learned from Team Clean!

TAKE NOTE…

Let's figure out what you need to clean each week! (Make notes below.)

Floor surfaces

_____

_____

_____

_____

Bathrooms

_____

_____

_____

_____

Kitchen

_____

_____

_____

_____

Trash/Recycling

_____

_____

_____

_____

Dusting

_____

_____

_____

_____

Pet-Related Jobs

_____

_____

_____

_____

Weekly items to be addressed. (Does anything need to be changed, refilled weekly?)

_____

_____

_____

_____

Wish list (add it now!)

_____

_____

_____

_____

Now take a look at the jobs and see where equipment overlaps. It is best to have one person handle a piece of equipment. You don't want people waiting for someone else to finish in order to start their own jobs. Make your piles. Play around with them until they are even (or maybe in your case uneven, depending on the ages of your family members). Obviously, you need to make the number of piles the same as the number of people on your team. Once your piles seem right, go back and assign a name to each one.

Pile #1 – name _____

_____

_____

_____

_____

_____

Pile #2 – name _____

_____

_____

_____

_____

_____

_____

Pile #3 – name _____

_____

_____

_____

_____

_____

_____

Pile #4 – name _____

_____

_____

_____

_____

_____

_____

Pile #5 – name _____

_____

_____

_____

_____

Including Visitors—Fans

●●●●●●●●●●●●●●●●●●●●●●●●●●●●●●●●●●

"Children are not casual guests in our home. They have been loaned to us temporarily for the purpose of loving them and instilling a foundation of values on which their future lives will be built."
– James Dobson

● ● ●

It may seem crazy, but our kids' friends love to clean our house! Of course, when their parents hear what they are doing, I am not sure they are quite so happy. From the beginning of Team Clean, it has always been a rule that if you are at our house on a Thursday night, you must participate in Team Clean. Since Team Clean is on a school night, most nights it is just our family. There are nights, however, over the summer and during the holidays when friends are over, so they are expected to participate.

The first visitor, I believe, was my oldest son's first girlfriend. She was a sophomore in high school. We gave her the job of vacuuming. I refused to let my husband give her the toilets…although he tried.

My kids tell me that on Thursdays, their friends ask on Facebook whether "Team Clean is on tonight" and can they "come do Team Clean." One of my son's friends came over to do Team Clean when my son wasn't even home yet! We gave him the assignment of my son's room. He cleaned that room better than anyone ever had.

• •

"The most surprising thing I have seen from Team Clean is the participation from my friends.. I would like to think that they just love my family; however, I would be lying to myself if I did not admit that it could be the food."

-Bucky

our son– started Team Clean at age 10

• •

Including our kids' friends in Team Clean has made us get to know their friends better and come to really enjoy having them around. It has even made our children get to know each other's friends better.

• •

"I did Team Clean a lot, several times in fact. I just love food. I'll do anything for food. Isn't that what Team Clean is all about?"

-Mike Holt

• •

Over the years, we have had more than twenty-five different visitors join us for Team Clean. We have even had people who have lived with us for periods of time who have become part of the regular routine. My oldest son, Stephen, lived in Germany for a year after he graduated from high school, so he made many German friends. Occasionally, one of his German friends makes a trip to the U.S. and stays with us for a night or two. One guy, Jan, had an internship and needed to stay with us for a few weeks. Of course, we explained to him that he would be part of Team Clean for the time he was here. During his first Team Clean, Jan ruined his favorite shorts with bleach, and we felt terrible. We thought he must hate Team Clean. We never mentioned the ritual again. A week went by, and on his second Thursday staying with us, he came home from his internship and rang the doorbell. My husband answered the door and the first words out of Jan's mouth were a very excited, "Team Clean!" He then ran into the kitchen, and in his beautiful German accent, he asked, "Is it time to start Team Clean?" He swears that he plans to teach his family in Germany all about Team Clean.

• •

"During my stay at Carol's house, Carol asked me to participate in Team Clean. To me, helping with the housework while enjoying all the advantages that come along with living with a family came naturally. In fact, I think excluding a member of the family from doing the housework, even a very temporary member, would probably have led to me feeling exactly this way: excluded. Thus, Team Clean was a welcome opportunity to give something back in return for the family hospitality. To be honest, Team

Clean never felt like doing hard work or any kind of work worth shirking. The work did not take very long since it was split up between every family member. And the nice dinner afterward with the whole family immediately made me feel connected to the family. Team Clean really made me feel welcome and part of the household. In my short time with the Pauls, I bonded with all of them through Team Clean!"

-Jan Olbrich

"Team Clean Visitor"

• •

My nephews have permanent jobs that are theirs when they are here. They beg their mom and dad to start Team Clean at their house. My one nephew even keeps Team Clean clothes of his own here!

This is the list of guests who have participated in our Team Clean:

- Marissa—Hyattsville, MD

- Jimmy—Baltimore, MD

- Mary—Cuxhaven, Germany

- Tommy—Crofton, MD

- Elise—Bowie, MD

- Kelly—Cape St. Claire, MD

- Alicia—Bowie, MD

- Adam—Clarksville, MD

- Mike—Greenbelt, MD

- Nick—Gambrills, MD

- Brian—Gambrills, MD

- Jacob—Bowie, MD

- Chelsea—Brentwood, MD

- Lauren—Grasonville, MD

- Will—Hyattsville, MD

- Patti—Crofton, MD

- Lisa—Greensboro, NC

- Peter—Grasonville, MD

- Jan—Düsseldorf, Germany

- Kevin—Gambrills, MD

- Caitlin—Gambrills, MD

- Matt—Bowie, MD

- Dave—Bowie, MD

- Tom—College Park, MD

● ●

"I remember Team Clean! I just remember how you guys somehow made cleaning fun. And I feel like it also somehow bonded you guys as a family because everyone wanted to be home to do chores—which is pretty unheard of if you ask me."

-Elise O'Meara

"Team Clean Visitor"

● ●

Our daughter never quite savored Team Clean the way the rest of us do. She was there to get her job done and move on. She is now away at college and not only does she not come home for Team Clean (understandable), but she is quite offended when we add her to the chart when she is home for holidays! She has tried to negotiate with us, explaining that she is now a guest. Luckily, guests have always been expected to participate, so that argument doesn't get far!

● ● ●

Moving Beyond Housework—Creating a Family Tradition

"Little things make the big things happen."
– **John Wooden**

● ● ●

Think of Team Clean like any other family tradition. Take for example Thanksgiving. Odds are you do something close to the same thing each Thanksgiving. That's what makes it special! Some of our best memories of growing up are normally from the annual traditions of our childhood. Team Clean is a tradition you are building for your family. (And you are getting a clean house each week as a bonus!)

For most Thanksgiving dinners to happen each November, it takes a lot of work. Someone has to go out and buy all the food, unload it, and put it all away, prepare it, cook it, clean the house (well, in families that don't do Team Clean), set the table, reheat food, serve the food, do all those dishes, and put away leftovers. Yet, when we talk about the holiday, we talk about how great it was to spend time with everyone and we focus on the visit, the fun, the traditional family dishes and the "togetherness." Nobody would ever think of skipping Thanksgiving just to avoid washing a dish or two. The holiday has come to be too special for them. This is much like what you will see Team Clean become if you build it into your family tradition.

My "smart husband" realized before Team Clean was even born that there was more to it than a clean house. He wanted Team Clean to be a family night. We wanted Team Clean to be one of our family traditions. We wanted not only to get a clean house each week, but we wanted to start a weekly family ritual that included dinner and an activity. We knew that because it was a school night, adhering to the right schedule was key.

TEAM CLEAN SCHEDULE

If you were organizing any holiday or family event, you would plan out the evening, and Team Clean is no different. Picking your night is not the end of scheduling. The night itself needs to go according to a scheduled plan. Start the cleaning about an hour to an hour and a half before you want to sit down to your activity/dinner. You will get quicker the longer you do this. The cleaning part of our Team Clean takes about thirty minutes now. We recommend you start Team Clean at 6:00 or 6:30, clean for an hour or so, and order the dinner at 7:30 so you can start your dinner and activity at 8:00. Remember to include the ordering and picking up of dinner in the cleaning part of your timing so your food is ready when it is time to eat. When our kids were young, we tried to order from places that delivered. As we gained drivers in the family, we added "picking up dinner" to the job chart.

Even if the schedule slips, you can be in bed by 9:30 (it is a school and work night after all). Pick the times that work for you. Obviously with little kids, you need to finish by bedtime, so start early enough to finish on time. And be consistent with the schedule as well as the night. The kids will take to Team Clean easier if they can count on it being the same each week. Finally, and this may seem obvious, but be sure to do the cleaning first! Even the best of kids (and spouses) will be tempted to try to find a way out of cleaning if they have already enjoyed the reward.

• •

"It was that night—all working together as one team—that we were able to clean the house in approximately an hour."
-Stephen
our son – started Team Clean at age 13

• •

Just like you would with any family event, give kids warnings that it is "almost time to go" or that they "need to get ready." The more reminders and hints that "Team Clean is tonight" or "about to start," the better. Put the chart and highlighter on the counter at start time and call in the troops. Your holiday is about to begin.

To make Team Clean a Family Tradition and not just a weekly way to get the house clean, make sure to keep the cleaning part and the family dinner/activity part equal when it comes to time spent.

TEAM CLEAN DINNER

From day one, we all picked something to do together once our jobs were complete. We have always done the cleaning part of Team Clean during the dinner prep hour, so from the very first days of our ritual, we decided it made sense to order takeout or delivery for our meal that night. Ordering takeout was something we rarely did at the time, so when we announced this part to the kids, it was considered a real treat. The dinner is a big part of Team Clean. For some of our kids, this is the most important part! Eating the dinner together is one of the things that makes Team Clean a family night. Plan the dinner in advance. Pick a dinner that is a treat for everyone—something everyone will look forward to. We get takeout every week, and it is special to our family since Team Clean night is the only day of the week that we order out. When we first started Team Clean, we figured that we were ordering out once a week anyway, just on various nights depending on our schedules. So when we decided to order on Team Clean night, we stopped ordering any other days. So it really had no impact on the family budget; we just shifted to ordering on the same night rather than sporadically. Ordering out serves not only as a treat, but it gives the cook or cooks in the family the night off from cooking, which leaves plenty of time for cleaning! Another benefit to ordering out is that it frees up the kitchen for cleaning. It is hard to get the kitchen properly cleaned if the cleaner is trying to work around a cook, pots, dishes, and food in various stages of preparation. If you think about this from the parents' point of view, you are replacing cooking and dinner cleanup time with this new weekly cleaning time; it's really just a trade-off!

Ordering takeout has worked for our family, but it is not the only option. If your family enjoys going out for a meal, by all means consider that option. It takes more time and generally costs a little more, but if it works for you, then do it. If this is your option, then dining out would probably end up being the family activity.

• •

"One member of the team got to choose where we ordered dinner from each week. It was like Christmas when it was your night to order. And everyone had to agree with it no matter what."
-Kiersten
our daughter – started Team Clean at age 8

• •

If restaurant meals are not your thing due to budgetary reasons, health reasons, or some other reason, and you must cook, then plan carefully. Remember, it is difficult to clean the kitchen and cook at the same time. I would recommend having something premade that can easily be heated in the oven such as lasagna or a casserole. You could even try a one-pot meal such as chili that can be heated in a Crockpot off to the side and out of the way. Maybe Team Clean night could be when you get something from the grocery store that you would normally tell your kids they couldn't have or maybe you just add a special dessert to a normal meal. But remember to make the meal something special and not something you would routinely have on another night, and more importantly, establish the tradition of what your "special treat" is each week. Changing it up too much breaks the idea of the family tradition you are trying to establish.

TEAM CLEAN

Whatever you decide for the meal, if at all possible, let the kids trade off having some say each week in the food choice. Allowing the kids a night where they get to choose the meal puts them in a semi-leadership role on Team Clean. It keeps them from just seeing themselves as workers.

Also, we all know everyone likes to pick out food... why do you think Subway and Chipotle are so popular...people get to point and pick!

TEAM CLEAN ACTIVITY

To make Team Clean a bonding experience, we chose an activity to do while we ate the "ordered out food." Since the whole family loved watching the show *Survivor*, we all agreed to make our weekly ritual watching the show together. This quickly became something we shared as a family. We talked about the people like we knew them. We gave *Survivor* T-shirts to each other as gifts. We even made it one of the new games at our school's annual carnival that we run. We can now go back over the years and talk about our favorite seasons, favorite survivors, etc.

We thought to make watching *Survivor* our Team Clean family activity because it happened to air on the night we did Team Clean. But, as shows tend to do, after a few years, it changed nights! At first, we were lost—what would we do for Team Clean? We had been doing Team Clean on Thursdays for so long that no one wanted to change nights. The new (to us at the time) DVR technology saved us. We simply learned to record the series at the beginning of each season so we could then watch the show on our schedule. We quickly found added benefits: We can fast-forward through the commercials, pause when we need to, and even adjust our evening schedule to a slightly later time as our kids grow older and practices and school nights run later. So keep in mind when planning your activity that you do not have to be limited to what is on television that night, or even what is on television at a certain time if that is the activity you choose for your family.

● ●

"Getting to watch Survivor and enjoy a nice burrito
from Chipotle is a great change of pace from the
boring school week."
-Charlie
our son – started Team Clean at age 4

● ●

The key to making the family activity and Team Clean successful is to pick an activity that everyone enjoys and one that can include dinner. Having dinner take place during the show or game or whatever else is chosen helps make sure all family members will be there. After all, the entire family will be excited about the dinner since they will have worked up an appetite doing their cleaning jobs. It may sound hard finding an activity that appeals to everyone since ages are going to vary and so will interests, but with a little thought, you will find what is right for your family.

• •

"One thing that has stayed consistent over the years is watching the show Survivor; it helps us get excited to do Team Clean because we get excited to finish our jobs, get the food, and sit down and watch."

-Bucky

our son – started Team Clean at age 10

• •

Some ideas to consider are:

- T.V. shows: Reality shows, such as *American Idol* or *Dancing with the Stars*, lend themselves to family viewing since they generally appeal to all ages, but sitcoms and dramas can work as well. You can even consider game shows—*Family Feud* is one that you can play along with and could be fun for the kids and parents.

- Movies: Watching a movie takes a little longer than a T.V. show, but if you time it right, it can be a great activity. The key is to have the movie pre-selected so you do not have to spend the entire activity time trying to find a movie that all can agree on (a seemingly impossible task for our family!). Ordering movies through your cable system or Netflix makes the choices almost limitless, and of course, you can watch them on your own schedule. I would advise having a system for selecting the movie such as rotating the selector each week or having the parents pick it.

- Games: Playing games as a family can be great fun, and there are many games that can be played and enjoyed by the whole family. But you should find one that can be completed within the time you have set aside for the activity. Games such as Risk and Monopoly are great, but they take some time to set up and can go on for extended periods of time. Our family has always loved to play Yahtzee together, even when the kids were so young they still needed help with adding up the dice. In fact, our youngest child learned addition from playing Yahtzee as a toddler.

- Cards: Everyone can get hooked on card games and there are many games that can be played with teams. And cards are played at a table, which makes eating the dinner while playing even easier. Cards are a perfect Team Clean activity because they go from toddler games of Go Fish to college age games of poker. Playing "Dealer calls" allows everyone to take turns in choosing the card game to be played. This activity will grow with your family!

Make your dinner and activity the same each week...
it's the only way to create a tradition!

Just like you might hear someone in late November telling his kids "Happy Thanksgiving" on a Thursday morning, my husband wakes the kids up on each Thursday morning in our house to "Happy Team Clean." Sometimes, he even can be heard saying, "Happy Team Clean Eve" on Wednesday.

● ●

"Team Clean is definitely a positive thing for every family. It is a time to bond with each other and get work done too."
-Charlie
our son – started Team Clean at age 4

● ●

The reward part of Team Clean is a big part of the bonding process, so don't skip it. Think about what works best for your family. Whether you watch your family's favorite TV show or play a favorite board game, make the activity the same every week. You are forming a tradition that your family will always remember. I never thought this would happen, but now our kids won't let *us* skip Team Clean!

TAKE NOTE...

Make notes of what your family already enjoys together... (Write down everything and anything.) This will help when it comes time to create your family tradition. It might help you choose special outfits or a song you play each week. You never know! So brainstorm now.

Just to get you going, think of...favorite songs, favorite vacations/ outings, favorite books/games/TV shows/movies, favorite characters, favorite holidays, favorite activities. What did you love as a kid that you might want to introduce to your family? Don't leave any ideas out!

_____

_____

_____

_____

_____

_____

_____

_____

_____

_____

_____

_____

_____

_____

_____

_____

_____

Establishing the Coach

● ●

"I've always found that the speed of the boss is the
speed of the team."
– Lee Iacocca

● ● ●

The coach of Team Clean should be the one who blindly believes in it! The one who plans to set a good example of persevering through the tough weeks and never giving up. He or she is the leader of Team Clean and will have an equal number of jobs (if not more). The coach will be the person who makes sure Team Clean becomes a tradition and never gets skipped. Make sure your coach helps pick the reward for your Team Clean.

I firmly believe that if both parents are not on board, Team Clean cannot work. (Unless, of course, only one parent lives in the home). I have a strong personality and I love to lead events. For fifteen years now, I have run huge events in our community. I run the registration for 2,500 campers every summer for our basketball camp.

But when it comes to Team Clean, my husband is the leader. There is no discipline like that of a father. A father's simple presence can often set the tone for good behavior. If my husband didn't lead our Team Clean, it would have died out within the first month.

My husband was the salesman of the whole idea. He had a quiet way of implementing it. But it worked! He never gave up. He plugged along even when some weeks didn't go as well as others. He refused to allow the tradition to end. For six weeks each year, the kids and I live on a college campus so I can run our family's basketball camp with my father and brother. For those six weeks, my husband actually does Team Clean alone each Thursday. As you can see, we have been blessed with a very good leader!

TEAM CLEAN

Bill Gates has said,
"Technology is just a tool. In terms of getting the kids together to work and motivating them, the teacher is most important."
We have all had bad teachers, average teachers, and great teachers. The great teacher makes all the difference in how the class performs. Make sure your Team Clean coach is ready to play the role of the best possible teacher.

People always work better for an active boss. When the boss is working hard and involved, the people under him/her stay dedicated and true to their jobs. They don't feel taken advantage of. As long as the boss is still working, there is no way to complain that things aren't fair. Who would the workers cry their unfairness pleas to? Bosses who demand the same of themselves as they do of their workers are the ones who get the best results. So, when parents have a rough day or a late meeting or don't feel well, they should treat themselves the same way they would one of the kids. They should start their jobs early or late and get them done! These tough nights are the nights when the reward is most gratifying!

Starting Team Clean is like starting any self-improvement activity. We exercise and eat right to look better and become stronger and more fit. We hit the pavement to look for a new job to better our careers, make more money, and enjoy what we do more. If the end result of working hard to better ourselves was not a good one that we looked forward to, we would throw in the towel pretty fast. The reward of Team Clean needs to be something that the coach looks forward to as much as the kids do.

It's important that the coach likes the reward of Team Clean. It will help him/her believe in keeping it alive. My husband always makes a cocktail for himself halfway through Team Clean and one for me too. This is his little tradition. I am normally cleaning some bathroom when in he comes with my drink! It is not hard to figure out a way to get every family member on board with this Team Clean idea. Just be creative and think about what is special to each person. If there is something your assistant coach would love to do each week, make it part of the Team Clean reward. Not only do players bond through this family ritual, but the coaches do too!

Coaching the Team—Getting the Family Team to Work

"Individual commitment to a group effort—that is what makes a team work, a company work, a society work, a civilization work."
– Vince Lombardi

• • •

My dad is a basketball coach, and he always says, "What makes basketball work makes life work." The hard work, sacrifice, and dedication that players bring to their teams, they soon learn to bring to all areas of their lives. Each of our children learned this through being a Team Clean "player." What makes a player succeed on any team is what makes him or her succeed at Team Clean: show up for practice and games, learn the fundamentals and practice them correctly, play for a positive coach, do your best, care about your team and team members, keep your priorities in order, and stay committed. If each person is fulfilling these requirements, the team works.

EVERYONE MAKES THIS TEAM!

When my daughter was starting her freshman year in high school, she decided to try out for field hockey. Since we had never had a child play fall sports in high school, we didn't know that tryouts take place in mid-August. We had booked our two-week family vacation at the beach. It was our first year being able to go for two full weeks, and we were all really looking forward to it. Four of my daughter's tryout days were during our beach vacation. The distance between her high school and the beach is 130 miles and the drive takes about two-and-a-half to three hours. We immediately decided to have her "commute." When the athletic director heard what we were doing, she suggested we have her stay with a friend or even her grandparents who live right near the school. I said, "But if Kiersten isn't there, then it wouldn't be family vacation."

Just like you can't have someone missing from family vacation, you can't have someone missing from Team Clean. All members of the "team" must be present—ALWAYS! Do not fall into the trap of letting people miss, even if it is for "a good reason." Everyone has thirty to sixty minutes to spare. Anyone who lives in the house should be expected to be part of Team Clean, even if he has to start early or late.

• •

"After all, everyone was working, so it was fair."

-Stephen

our son – started Team Clean at age 13

• •

100 PERCENT PARTICIPATION REQUIRED—NO SKIPPING WITHOUT A DOCTOR'S NOTE.

Each individual matters when it comes to Team Clean. He matters for the house to be cleaned, and he matters for all the other great things Team Clean brings.

Our children are not allowed to miss Team Clean. They know it is every Thursday. They have fair warning. It is not a surprise in their schedules. I have overheard my son tell my husband that he had a big test to study for, but my husband said to him, dead seriously, "Son, you know what comes first." My husband feels that one hour is all Team Clean takes and that is not going to ruin anything else in your life as long as you schedule your next most important priority correctly!

We demand the same commitment from ourselves. Both parents have to be involved and present a true belief in Team Clean for it to work. I have seen families try to implement Team Clean and let one parent "sit out," but it never works. I have seen it done even when Dad or Mom was at work (a legitimate excuse), but it still doesn't work. Plan your work schedule around Team Clean if necessary. My husband frequently gets asked to attend evening meetings for work. He blocks his calendar on Thursday nights as "scheduled." This commitment reminds him to try his hardest to get the meetings scheduled for any night but Thursday. If he really gets stuck, he attends the meeting and then comes in and starts his Team Clean a little late, just as if he got out of football practice late. If kids don't get a legitimate excuse, Mom and Dad shouldn't either.

Everyone must always do the job he or she is assigned. If we know someone has a late practice or something big going on, we might move a few jobs around so that person's workload is really light, but we always include the person. It is important that everyone knows you can't skip Team Clean. No one can think of it as an option. It doesn't take long for it to become second nature that every member of the family participates in Team Clean. They accept it as part of their schedules, like going to school or sports practice. As long as you stay consistent!

● ●

"Everyone had to participate, including any friends who might be over."

-Kiersten

our daughter – started Team Clean at age 8

● ●

COACH WITH PATIENCE AND BE POSITIVE, NOT NEGATIVE

Our youngest was four when we started Team Clean. Our daughter was seven. Our two older boys were ten and thirteen. In the beginning years, we assigned our younger children one parent as their "supervisor." They were still on the chart and had their job lists just like normal, but it was the supervisor's job to teach them their jobs and make sure the jobs were being done and being done right. Team Clean takes a while to train. Have patience and don't judge the job too harshly. They will get better. Positive reinforcement is the key. If all children hear is what they are doing wrong and they can't see any success in the future, they will stop trying to improve.

When my daughter was in fifth grade, I started a school dance team for her age group. I coached it with two nineteen year olds from my neighborhood. I remember one day one of my nineteen year old assistants was irritated with the kids and in a stern voice said, "I am going to go around the room and tap the shoulder of every girl who is not smiling." After she said it, I told her she could have said, "I am going to go around the room and tap the shoulder of every girl who *is* smiling!" The request would have been the same. The way it was presented would have been completely different. I may be going out on a limb here, but I would bet that the results would be better using the latter method.

It is very tempting to criticize (especially if you are a perfectionist). But as long as kids are doing their jobs and playing their positions, let it be. Things don't have to be perfect!

BE CONSISTENT

When we first started Team Clean, we would look at everyone's schedule for the week and then pick the night that seemed to work the best. It turned out that there was never a night that was perfect according to the family's varied schedules, but we tried. One week, Team Clean was a Monday, and the next, it could be a Wednesday. Scheduling Team Clean seemed harder than doing Team Clean. And the kids had no idea when it was coming. When they would come home from school or practice, it would be sprung on them without warning, making it hard for them to adjust. We soon learned that Thursdays generally worked best, and we decided to set this day in stone as Team Clean night. Team Clean is now on a Thursday night and the day has never changed. We think it is a great start to the weekend. It means the house is ready for anything we want to do over the weekend. We can have guests over (without the pre-arrival cleaning panic), do a project, go out with friends, relax, or travel to the beach because the cleaning is done. We only move Team Clean once a year. We all do Team Clean on Wednesday the week of Thanksgiving.

Keeping Team Clean on the same night or day is important because, after a while, you will learn to schedule around it. I started a youth group at our church a few years ago, and when it came time to pick the night, Thursday seemed the most logical. It was closest to the weekend so teens were almost done with school for the week, yet they wouldn't be out doing their weekend plans. I knew I could not commit because of the conflict with Team Clean. We chose Wednesday as our youth group night all because of our Team Clean, and it still is held on Wednesdays to this day. You have to think like this. Hold Team Clean in your calendar like you would a doctor's appointment. If people ask whether you are available, you need to say, "Oh, that's our family night; is there another time that works?"

● ●

"I always knew what I had to do on Thursdays."

-Charlie

our son– started Team Clean at age 4

● ●

DON'T FORFEIT ANY GAMES!

Every day you get up, shower, and make yourself presentable. Some days you might enjoy this and do a great job of it; other days, you rush through it and could care less how you look, but either way, you have accepted it as part of your routine. Each evening, you might be the one who makes dinner. Some nights you might go all out and the meal is amazing while other nights, you throw together whatever you can find just to get a meal on the table. You may not always be in the mood to cook, but you get dinner going either way. This is how Team Clean works. Some weeks, you will be tempted to skip Team Clean. Sometimes, you will think, "Maybe we could put it off until the weekend." You will be tired, and the last thing you will want to do is clean, much less get the family cleaning. Don't give in to this temptation. It is better to do a half-hearted job than to skip. The sooner you make Team Clean a weekly norm, the easier it will run. After a while, Team Clean will seem so easy that you will start to think of it as merely a family night and barely realize there is even a cleaning segment to it!

THE ASSISTANT COACH COMES CLEAN

I am going to come clean and admit something. My family won't even know this unless this book goes to print. So for now, it is just a small secret with my computer. When I feel like I don't have the time to finish my jobs, I hold the master bathroom shower for the next day. Besides running out of time, I have even done this for the sake of a cleaner house. There have been times when I have thought, "Boy, the shower is getting bad; I want to spend extra time on it." So my "putting it off until tomorrow" decision was for the sake of a cleaner shower! Did I convince you?

Normally, I have to say, this has worked out fine. But there was one time that I regretted it. My husband went golfing with three of his friends and they came back to our house afterwards. The food was amazing, the house looked great, and the drinks were cold. When they arrived, they were sweaty from a day of golf in 90-degree weather, and they all needed to take showers. Even though I had "postponed" my cleaning of the shower, I wasn't worried because I figured the guys would use the guest bathroom. My husband told them to use any place they wanted, and of course, our OCD friend chose our shower. A few months later when we all got together again, he gave me advice on keeping a shower clean!

TEAM CLEAN

Every kid can't make every team. In fact some kids can't make any team. This is a shame because a lot can be learned from being on a team. This is your chance to ensure your kids play for at least one team in life and reap the benefits and all the valuable lessons that come from being a member (plus think about the relationship you are building between them as siblings—teammates bond in a very special way).

Keeping Up—
Quarterly Cleaning Jobs

"Inch by inch, life's a cinch. Yard by yard, it's really hard."
– Anonymous

• • •

Team Clean never takes us more than an hour to do. I think the reason for this is because we did the initial decluttering of our whole house and also because we have a quarterly cleaning regiment. During Team Clean, we can be quick. We are cleaning surfaces that we know we cleaned the week before, and that we know we will clean again the following week. We don't have to move clutter or furniture for the most part, and we are "in and out" of each space easily. There is never built-up dirt. The tougher jobs and the ones that take longer are not addressed during Team Clean. And that's what keeps it to an hour or less of actual cleaning.

Four times each year, we deep clean in order to allow Team Clean to remain a "surface cleaning" job. We chose to base our quarterly cleaning times around our major family events and holidays. This schedule has allowed us to have the house looking its best when we need it to. As you can see, we continue to declutter spaces three times a year.

QUARTERLY CLEANING JOBS

Quarter 1: March (Easter or Spring Cleaning)

Like most people, we love spring. It a time for new growth and new beginnings. (And the first nice days at the beach!) Reward yourself and put up a spring door decoration after this three-step deep clean.

1. Clean the kitchen floor: Although you will vacuum and spot clean the kitchen floor weekly, it does need a thorough cleaning every so often. Be sure to remove chairs, small furniture, and area rugs so you can get at the whole floor unobstructed.

2. Declutter bulk items and dispose: Bigger items such as old furniture and large toys can be harder to get rid of and so tend to collect in corners of the house and garage. Look for these things and find a way to dispose of them by either lugging them to the dump, selling them on eBay, or giving them to the thrift store. Some organizations will come pick them up right from your front porch.

3. Clean/organize the garage: Most garages attract junk and clutter, and if not addressed, will render the garage useless. Find a place for things you need to keep and discard what is being stored for no real reason. If you need to, re-read the declutter chapter and quickly declutter again in any rooms that have started to get out of control.

Quarter 2: June (School's Out and the Family's Annual Crabfeast)

We traditionally celebrate the end of the school year and the beginning of summer with a big crabfeast with all of our family and friends. It's great fun, and we use this event as motivation to get some other larger cleaning items done. I used to take on a huge home renovation project each year to make the house look its best, so this three-step deep clean seems like easy prep for the party now.

1. Clean the kitchen floor: Yes, this should be done again.

2. Touch up/paint the walls: Common area walls such as hallways, foyers, and stairwells tend to get smudges, fingerprints, and other scuffs and marks. It is amazing what kind of dirt small kids can put on walls. It is impractical to paint the whole rooms and hallways routinely, but you can go over the dirt with fresh paint and make the area look as if it had been repainted. Be sure to use the same paint that the wall was originally painted with to get a perfect blend of color and use a roller rather than brush to avoid brush strokes.

3. Steam clean carpets: Most carpets need to be steam cleaned once per year to stay looking new. We rent a commercial steamer from an area store and can get the entire house done in a day. The rental and cleaner costs about $50.00 so it is much cheaper than hiring a professional. But if your carpets are in really bad condition from kids and pets, then a professional cleaning will probably get them looking better than the do-it-yourself route.

Quarter 3: September (Back to school)

Every September, I get the itch to reorganize and get back on schedule. This three-step deep clean really helps me get started. There is not a lot to do this quarter, so we do the least fun job—cleaning windows!

1. Clean the kitchen floor: Yet again!

2. Clean/organize the garage: Our garage needs decluttering twice a year. I am a thrift store junkie (and a "see it on the side of the road…I have to stop and pick it up" junkie). If your garage is still clean from the spring, you get to skip this chore!

3. Wash windows inside and out: Nobody likes to wash windows, but this step is necessary. Dirty windows make a house grungy, not to mention the difficulty in seeing outside. Clean windows make the house shine. If you have newer windows, cleaning is fairly easy from the inside—just tilt them in and spray with glass cleaner and wipe. Always have enough rags on hand so you are wiping with a dry rag to prevent streaks. If you need to wash the outside of the windows from the outside (older windows), a squeegee with a telescoping extension pole works great. You can get poles long enough to extend to the second floor, thus eliminating ladders.

Quarter 4: December (Holidays!)

Be sure to do these jobs before the decorations go up. The decorations will not be in the way as you clean, and when they do go up, the house will look the best it's looked all year!

1. Clean and/or refinish kitchen floor: Our kitchen and foyer floors are hardwood with polyurethane finish that protects them from damage. The finish tends to dull, and even after a good cleaning, can look unimpressive. So once per year, we not only clean, but we add a refresher coat of finish. To do this, we buy a wood floor cleaner that has the refinisher in it. You apply the cleaner with a kitchen mop and it dries in about an hour or less. Ceramic tile floors may need the grout cleaned and sealed, and other types of floors may need a good buffing. Giving your floors the attention they need really makes the house sparkle for the holidays just in time for friends and family.

2. Clean and touch up paint on trim and doors: The trim, molding, and most of the doors in our house are white, and they attract scuffs, dirt, and fingerprints. Most of these marks can be cleaned with bleach cleaner and a damp rag. But to make these areas look like new, I get the paintbrush and paint can out to go over what does not wipe off. We keep the same brand of paint in our work closet at all times so it blends perfectly when spot painting. And since everything is white, it means one paint can and dirty brush for the entire house, making this a quick and easy job that shows big results.

3. Clean light fixtures: Light fixtures and ceiling fans attract a lot of dust, and since they are generally beyond reach, they usually do not get dusted as part of the normal dust routine. Now is the time to remedy this. Be sure to clean clear glass fixtures with glass cleaner to get a "like new" shine. And use a stepladder for easy access to high places. Standing on a kitchen chair is dangerous and will only encourage you to do a rushed

and sloppy job. You will be amazed at how new and bright the house looks with shiny light fixtures.

4. Sort closets and drawers and dispose of unwanted items: We do this process before Christmas to make room for the new stuff. It means a lot to give away items before Christmas, knowing they might really help someone who needs the item as a gift for her family/children. It also lets you see just how much your family really needs to be given and what they have room for.

In business, they say you can tell a lot about someone by looking at his smile (teeth), grooming (hands), and shoes (shined). When it comes to your house, you give the impression it is clean when the walls, windows, and floors look good. Do not neglect the quarterly deep cleaning jobs. It can be very frustrating to clean the house every week and not have it actually look clean when you are done. If this is happening, it is probably because the house is recluttering, the carpets are getting dirty, the walls are smudged, and you can't see out the windows.

But the *real* reason to keep up with the quarterly cleaning jobs is because it's the only way to keep Team Clean under an hour each week. It is because of these deep cleans and keeping up with clutter control that you will find you rarely have to scrub anything.

The quarterly cleaning is what keeps the cleaning portion of the weekly Team Clean to under an hour.

Of course we have a chart for our quarterly cleaning jobs!

QUARTERLY CLEANING JOBS:

Quarter 1: March (Easter)

1. Refinish kitchen floor

2. Declutter bulk items and dispose

3. Clean/organize the garage

Quarter 2: June (Crabfeast)

1. Refinish kitchen floor

2. Touch up paint on the walls

3. Steam clean carpets and steps

Quarter 3: September (Back to school)

1. Refinish kitchen floor

2. Clean/organize garage

3. Wash windows inside and out

Quarter 4: December (Christmas)

1. Refinish kitchen floor

2. Touch up paint on trim

3. Clean light fixtures

4. Sort closets and drawers and dispose of unwanted items

Taking It on the Road

● ●

Let's get this show on the road.

– Anonymous

● ● ●

We go to our beach house a lot. We own the house with my parents so we have to be fair about the condition we leave it in when we head home. My parents hire a cleaner to clean after they leave. We have chosen to make it a habit just to clean on our own before leaving. One August, I stressed myself out and ruined the last day of vacation trying to get the house perfect before we headed home. I never went to the beach that day; I stayed back and played martyr. I felt so sorry for myself that I had to clean up the week's worth of filth while they had a blast on the beach. Of course, at the end of the day, they all told me how they had planned to help, but they were waiting until it was really time to leave. Yeah right! On my way home, I decided it was time to make a Team Clean BEACH Chart. It was a no brainer. The reward would be stopping for food on the way home! What a tool our family had developed. I felt blessed.

● ●

We soon learned to use this system
wherever we went...checking out at the
lake, leaving camp each summer, etc.
My husband even took our system so far
as to make a chart for the kids when
they went off to college, entitled "How To
Make The Honor Roll."

● ●

TEAM CLEAN
YACHT-SEA BEACH HOUSE:

EVERYONE:

- Bring your towel(s) (beach and/or bath) to the washer

- Bring your sheets/pillowcases to the upstairs closet

- Bring your box of personal items to the laundry room closet

Jobs

Bucky	Vacuum Rugs	Cover Grill			
Charlie	Vacuum Porch	Vacuum Bathroom Floor	Vacuum Hallway	Vacuum Kitchen Floor	Vacuum Laundry Room
Carol	Bring Dry Foods to Closet, Inventory	Straighten Whole House, Make Beds	Master Bath	Mop Porch	Yellow Bath
Kiersten	Wash Towels	1/2 Bath Toilet, Sink, Mirror	Den Bath Toilet, Sink, Mirrors		
Steve	Kitchen	Fridge	2nd Fridge		
Stephen	Put Bikes Away, Clean Shed	Clean Outdoor Shower	Put Chairs, Surfboards Away, Clean Surf Closet	Trash	

Convincing Dad to Get Involved

. . . .

"Our most basic instinct is not for survival but for family. Most of us would give our own life for the survival of a family member, yet we lead our daily life too often as if we take our family for granted."
– Paul Pearshall

• • •

Making every person who lives in your house participate in Team Clean is one of the key elements to establishing your tradition. If you are a two-parent household, both parents need to be on board. Most dads are not going to be excited about helping start this weekly ritual; odds are, up until now, they have not had to do the majority of cleaning, if any at all. They have most likely left the day-to-day discipline of the kids and organization of the home up to you. Dad needs to know that by choosing to become part of Team Clean, he is establishing himself as the leader of your home in a natural way. (Ironically, even if Mom leads Team Clean, kids see Dad as the leader.) Make sure to conduct your very first Team Clean *with* Dad! Your children will respond better and fight this new system a lot less. How do you nudge him to say, "Yes"?

- Have him read this chapter (my husband's point of view)

- Have him read Paul Pearshall's quote at the beginning of this chapter

- Show him the testimonials from the coaches on the back of the book. (If they believe in Team Clean, maybe he will too!)

- Have him look at families who are struggling with tough teenagers, and explain to him that establishing a tradition that instills discipline in your kids might cost him an hour per week now, but it could save him years of stress and worry later!

- Have him read our four kids' chapters to see what his kids could be saying about him in a few years!

AND NOW FROM DAD HIMSELF...

Most guys I know are just like me when it comes to housework; they are as excited about cleaning as they are about going to the opera or getting an invitation to a couples baby shower. With long days at work and helping out more and more with the kids, from diaper changing, to car pooling, to coaching their sports teams, it would seem like the last thing we men want to do is clean the house. We think we don't like to clean, and even if we did, there is really no time to do it.

But really, we can always find time for what is important in life, and having a clean, well run house is important. I caught on to the significance of Team Clean quickly. It was obvious that the rewards far outweighed the effort. Let's face it; cleaning once a week for an hour or less is not that hard. And once it becomes routine, it is no bother at all.

The little effort reaps huge returns. You will see the kids acting like a team, learning basic life skills (cleaning is a necessary skill), getting organized, and taking pride in their contributions to the household. In this day and age of constantly being in front of an electronic screen, Team Clean gets everyone, parents included, away from the screens, at least for a little while. Team Clean forces interaction among family members that may not occur otherwise. This interaction is the real reward of Team Clean.

But there are many other smaller returns as well. The house really is cleaner and more organized, which makes it more comfortable and inviting to live in. Even slobs enjoy a clean house more than a messy, dirty one.

Team Clean eliminates the nagging from the wife, or at least the nagging about cleaning up the mess. This one area of stress in the household is greatly reduced. The tension of who is doing more or less than his or her share of the housework is solved.

Just think about the amount of money that is saved by not getting a maid. It is easy to spend $6,000.00 to $8,000.00 a year on a weekly maid service. You can take a two-week family vacation for less than that! Once you start Team Clean and see how easy it is, you will be kicking yourself for ever having spent a dime paying someone to clean your house.

Team Clean is more than just cleaning the house. It is a special family night that includes a good meal, family togetherness, and a fun activity. I really look forward to it. It is a great break from the repetitiveness of the work night/school night routine of car pools, practices, homework, a rushed dinner, and bedtime. When I'm halfway through the cleaning part of the evening, I usually crack a beer or fix myself a nice cocktail and enjoy the evening. I fix one for my wife as well, and then we can both relax and enjoy the evening.

So put some effort into starting Team Clean. Your effort and attitude can be the difference between a great success and a total failure. If left to the mom alone, the system is much less likely to work. It is not fun for anyone to have the wife and mom nagging, pushing, and pleading with everyone to do his or her job. Lead by example and the nagging won't be necessary. If the kids see their dad doing housework, they will do it too. You will see soon enough that you are doing yourself and your family a great favor.

● ●

"My dad loves 'To Do' lists."
-Stephen
our son – started Team Clean at age 13

● ●

Hearing What Our Four Kids Have to Say

"It is easier to build strong children than to repair broken men."
– Frederick Douglass

• • •

STEPHEN

Stephen is the oldest of our four children. He was thirteen years old when we started Team Clean. We have assigned him many different jobs through our years of doing Team Clean. He has pretty much done every job on the chart! He missed a lot of Team Cleans over the years from living overseas at times, and I thought maybe he didn't quite get the bonding part of it because of that. I now see that Team Clean is a great way to draw your grown-up kids back home (free food), and the bonding never really ends. (This is really nice for younger siblings who can end up being that lone child stuck with Mom and Dad in the later years!)

• •

"The whole is greater than the sum of its parts."
– Aristotle

Being the oldest child, I can still remember when our most re-current family tradition began. It was the fall of my eighth grade year, and it arose rather serendipitously and surreptitiously. My parents may maintain that they intentionally formulated this idea in detail before we started, but the fact is, they stumbled upon it one day when they discovered the house was overrun with clutter and that basic cleaning duties had been skipped for some time. In order to get things clean faster, they asked us to lend a hand as they put things back into order. We agreed and all spent time doing various chores that were assigned to us. (My dad loves "To Do" lists.) That's when it happened: The synergy of "Team Clean" was realized.

At first, we children did not suspect anything unusual and cer-tainly did not grasp that a tradition was arising. We helped out that first day by doing various chores, which we usually did on our own (albeit reluctantly) when asked. However, it was that night—all working together as one team—that we were able to clean the house in approximately an hour, with no one ob-jecting. After all, everyone was working, so it was fair. Our parents rewarded us by ordering food from a local restaurant, and we watched our favorite TV show as a family while we ate.

Soon thereafter, my mom came up with the name *Team Clean*. (She was very proud of the slant rhyme she created.) My dad told us that cleaning as a team would be a weekly occurrence; he made a list of tasks, and he told us we would order from a restaurant of our choosing and eat while watching our favorite TV show *Survivor*. Team Clean was born.

We didn't object for a few reasons: First, they were our parents, and we kind of had to listen to them. Secondly, we liked to order food and watch TV. Lastly, we were all in this *together*. Certain aspects of Team Clean have changed over the years as we have gotten older. For example, we used to rotate jobs, but later, we decided to keep jobs constant, so everyone knew exactly what he or she would be going to do each week. This plan works as long as everyone agrees on his or her jobs. We also had to adapt as some children went to college or on trips, but it always seemed to work out. No matter what has changed, the general idea and efficiency have remained intact. Cleaning is no different from other team-related activities. Cleaning together can create a synergistic effect that no parent or set of parents can match on their own.

I have even taken the idea of Team Clean outside my immediate family. When I obtained my first post-collegiate job, I moved into a family-style home with four other young professionals. Unfortunately, none of them had been brought up in the same environment as I had; in fact, most had not cleaned at all or did not even know how to clean certain things in the house. However, since they were unwilling to pay for a maid service, they acquiesced to my suggestion that we choose one day to clean together. We chose Sunday as our day since we were not working at the office and tended to make a little mess on Friday and Saturday nights, which we did not want to remain throughout the week. Moreover, if a roommate were to go away for a weekend, it still worked because that person did not (theoretically) contribute to the weekend mess. Not only did we keep our house clean and in order, but cleaning also strengthened our bond as housemates. We still clean together every Sunday, and, even at age twenty-five, whenever I happen to be home at the parents' house on Thursday Team Clean Night, I still participate in our perennial family tradition.

BUCKY

· ·

Bucky is our second son. He was ten years old when we started Team Clean. He has always held the job of vacuuming the rugs throughout our years of doing Team Clean. He loves knowing what his job is and what he is responsible for. He used to watch his "own show" during the family part of Team Clean, but slowly came around to being the biggest advocate of Team Clean in the end!

· ·

"That rug really tied the room together."
– The Big Lebowski

Team Clean…yes the name sounds a bit cheesy; heck, the entire concept does. But if you find yourself reading my words, then you have probably bought into it all. Which is good because that is all it takes. I have even gotten just about all my friends to buy in, everyone except my ex, but that's how I knew it was not meant to be. I am not sure when I first bought into the whole thing, or any of my siblings for that matter, but now doing Team Clean once a week just seems like second nature.

I can honestly say I look forward to doing Team Clean every week. It is like getting past hump day; once you get to it, the week seems to slide by. We have switched a few times between Wednesdays and Thursdays throughout, depending on people's schedules and the democratic process of the Paul household. Either day was fine with me, but I would just recommend doing it later in the week to have something to look forward to. One thing that has stayed consistent over the years is watching the show *Survivor*; it helps us get excited to do Team Clean because we get excited to finish our jobs, get the food, and sit down and watch. So if you really want to know who to thank for Team Clean, it is Jeff Probst.

The most surprising thing I have seen from Team Clean is the participation from my friends. I can easily count two handfuls of friends who have participated with my family, and even a couple who have taken it back to their own families. At first, I felt weird asking them to participate, but everyone seems to love it. I would like to think that they just love my family; however, I would be lying to myself if I did not admit that it could be the food. We also have been pretty easy on them; it is never a good idea just to spring Team Clean on someone. If someone gets cleaning toilets his first night, chances are he will be running.

I don't want to admit that my job is easy, but I wouldn't give it up easily. Unless you've worked in the hotel industry or some similar job, I have probably vacuumed more square feet of rugs in my life than anyone my age. My parents even got me the professional grade vacuum that you always see people running down the hotel hallway; in fact, when I pass a janitor or maid, I naturally feel like I should throw a wave out or give a head nod, like two motorcycles passing each other. Unfortunately, the hotel staff looks at me as if I am crazy and never shows me any love back.

I feel like a professional because I have never switched jobs doing Team Clean, and I think I am the only one in my family who can say that. My siblings will say that is because I run the house, but I think it is because I stay low key and just start working as soon as Team Clean begins every week. I cannot lie, though; I do get nervous when I start to hear some complaining going around about people's jobs not being fair. I feel a bit like a dictator who can't believe that he got all these people to buy in for all this time. I mean really, cleaning bathrooms, taking out trash, getting on your hands and knees and doing floors. By comparison, vacuuming is a breeze.

I truly cannot say that I have ever disliked Team Clean. Even if I am not at home, I will usually find a way to get home for it. I will find myself road biking a few towns over just to make it back to Team Clean. There is not one particular reason why it stands out for me, but it is mainly the combination of the entire thing.

I do not picture it as cleaning my house or vacuuming; it is so much more than that. Honestly, I think about it simply as Team Clean. I guess you could say that I bought in.

KIERSTEN

Kiersten is our third child and only daughter. She was eight years old when we started Team Clean. She wanted to try every job there was just to make sure nobody had a better job than she did. She took years to become a fan of Team Clean. She now encourages her siblings when they are tired and not up for doing their jobs. She has come to think Team Clean is a breeze and that it is the only way to go! Some weeks, she actually offers to do extra jobs when she finishes her own.

"Teamwork divides the tasks and multiplies the success."
– Author Unknown

Thursday nights were a big event in the Paul house. It was Team Clean. Everyone had to participate, including any friends who might be over. We were all given a job or a few jobs that had to be completed prior to the start of *Survivor*, my family's favorite television show. Along with *Survivor*, our reward for cleaning the entire house was that we got to order dinner out. This was a big deal to us kids; we *never* got to eat out. One team member got to choose where we ordered dinner from each week. It was like Christmas when it was your night to order. And everyone had to agree with it, no matter what. Because of ordering out and watching *Survivor* as a family, Team Clean was almost looked forward to. And I mean *almost* because, believe me, it was no day at the beach doing all those chores.

Team Clean all started because my parents did not like to spend money. They were frugal, or as I like to call it, cheap. My parents thought it was crazy to order a maid service when the whole family could pitch in and clean the house just as well. I'm not even exactly sure when Team Clean actually began. I just know it has been happening every Thursday since I can remember.

Choosing your job was the hardest part. If you wanted an easy job (like me), then that meant you had to do more of them. After being tired of doing so many smaller jobs, I told my parents I wanted to switch to something else. I remember when they let me start cleaning the bathrooms—what an exciting moment for any young child. I was so happy and thought this would be a much better job; however, I soon found out this was not the best solution. I wanted to switch again and again. I was never satisfied with the job I had. I always thought someone else's job was easier or better than mine. My family likes to tease me about this often, but hey, when you're a kid, you simply don't want to work.

I finally found a job I could handle and would not get bored with too quickly—vacuuming the hardwood floors. All I had to do was put my headphones on and the floors would be done before I knew it.

Although doing the actual cleaning was not the most fun part of Team Clean, it had many advantages. It was nice to have a clean house every week. No one likes to live in filth, and the amount of dirt that can accumulate from six people living in one house is no joke. Team Clean is serious business and must be done each week. We all knew this, and yet it was not easy to comprehend. I do remember the couple of rare times we hired a cleaning service when I was a child. I had to straighten up my room before the maids came. I thought this was strange because weren't they supposed to clean for me? Isn't that the whole point? So really even without cleaning as a family once a week, you still have to clean for the maids to come.

All of my friends knew Thursdays were never the day to go to the Paul house, but if any of them ended up here, they knew they had to clean. I had finally gotten into my groove and was vacuuming the floors each week, but if I had a friend over, I had to give her that job. I was forced to do something much worse like clean the bathrooms because, c'mon, you can't have your guest scrubbing your toilets for you. At the time, I did not understand this, but now it is clearer to me.

Looking back at Team Clean, I now realize how much it taught me and how great a tradition it is. It has taught me responsibility and a hard work ethic. Going off to college for the first time is really what made me understand this. I remember one of my roommates saying she didn't know how to clean, and I was SHOCKED. I had been cleaning since I was a child. How could she not know what to do? This idea was so foreign to me—especially since cleaning our dorm room was a piece of cake compared to cleaning a whole house. I'm so thankful to have been raised with Team Clean because now I know how to take care of the place I live in.

I know Team Clean will be something I have forever, and I will start it with my own family someday, but for right now, I am just living in a house with my friends. I wonder how they'll feel about instituting Team Clean.

CHARLIE

• •

Charlie is the youngest of our four children. He was four years old when we started Team Clean. He probably can't remember life before Team Clean. He carried trash bags around our house that were bigger than him in the early years. He is pretty much willing to do any job. He never really fights any job we assign him. He tends to rush through it quietly, though. He loves to hide when Team Clean is about to start!

• •

"The advantage of growing up with siblings is that you become very good at fractions."
– Robert Brault

Team Clean has been in my life for as long as I can remember. When I was little, I didn't understand that Team Clean was a unique thing to our family. When my friends would talk about maids stealing things from them, I wouldn't relate to it at all because I clean my own stuff. When we would talk about doing chores, my friends always complained about how unfair it was that they did work and didn't get anything in return. This is one of my favorite parts about Team Clean. When you are a little kid, doing chores isn't going to sound appealing no matter what. But when you know you have a pizza waiting for you when you are done, it makes it that much easier. I imagine my parents had an easier time getting me to do chores than my friends' parents.

I always knew what I had to do on Thursdays. I didn't much like doing the work, but it's all worth it in the end. Getting to watch *Survivor* and enjoy a nice burrito from Chipotle is a great change of pace from the boring school week. Not to mention, I get a clean house for the next week.

The only bad part of Team Clean is that I actually have to do work. I was never quite able to get this through my head when I was little. I would always delay the inevitable. If I just did the work, it would only take me thirty minutes, tops. But Team Clean when I was younger always took at least an hour. And that was with the easy jobs that little kids get! All I had to do was dust some stuff and wash a few windows that didn't even need to be cleaned. That just proves that the best way to do Team Clean is just to get it over with. There is nothing better than finishing early and watching everyone else struggle through their jobs.

While I was growing up, my family ate very healthy food. My lunches would consist of a turkey sandwich on whole wheat bread, some fruit, some kind of vegetable, and plain popcorn.

Needless to say, I always had the worst lunch out of all my class-mates. That's another reason why Thursday was so awesome. It was my one night to pig out and eat anything I wanted. Whether it was pizza, a burrito, or Chinese, it was all better than I was used to. I think that is why we never really argued about what to eat. We were all "up for anything."

As you get older, Team Clean definitely starts to get old. That's why we would change jobs up every now and then. It keeps things a little interesting because you don't have to scrub toi-lets every week. Maybe one month you have to scrub toilets; then the next, you vacuum the rugs. This also keeps things fair because one person isn't always stuck with the worst job. We would also trade jobs between the kids. If one kid hated one job and the other hated something else, they might trade jobs. If the two jobs weren't quite equal work, then you would trade multiple things. Once we even did a three-person trade.

The one thing my parents, especially my dad, didn't like was having friends over during Team Clean. That's why when par-ents did make the exception, it was very special. I would get so excited because my neighbor Jacob or my cousin Brian would be over. And they loved it too because they would get free food! It's funny how the entire attitude of the house changes when friends are over. There is no complaining, faking injuries, or making up homework to get out of jobs; just work. It was like everyone put up the illusion that we do this every week without even complaining once. The house was always much cleaner and everyone worked much more efficiently. I never understood why my parents didn't let us have friends over more often; everyone actually does his or her job when friends are over. It was probably because my parents were too cheap to buy them something to eat.

Team Clean is definitely a positive thing for every family. It is a time to bond with each other and get work done too. It prepares you for the day you have your own house to clean. If it were not for Team Clean, I wouldn't have the faintest clue how to clean a house. I would highly recommend giving Team Clean a try to any of my friends or anyone reading this.

• •

I didn't edit or alter my kids' chapters in any way. I wanted the "truth to be told." I do feel like I have to defend myself in two areas after reading them though! Bucky mentions that we switched between Wednesdays and Thursdays, and you have heard me hammer home the point that you have to stay with the same night no matter what. For ten years, we never switched nights; we held firm to Thursday night once we figured out it was the best one for us. I still think this was a key element. We do, now that the kids are older, allow them to propose Wednesday night as an option. They actually get group text messages going with each other from their jobs and school and check each other's schedules and go through the process of trying to hold

Team Clean each week on the night most kids can make it back home!

Charlie mentions job trades. For the most part, our chart and job assignments stayed the same over the years. If the kids were making trades behind our backs, well then, I guess they were learning a whole skill I never even knew about! Now that they are older and don't all live at home, we have different team members present each week. Twelve years in, we do have to "re-assign some positions" each week in order to cover the entire house.

These changes work now because the tradition is solid. But I still hold firm that changes are not a good thing in the beginning years!

You should also note Charlie's honesty about the faking of injuries and trying to get out of Team Clean. Our kids were not always excited about Team Clean, but we persevered!

Learning Lessons from Team Clean

• •

"Life is a succession of lessons which must be lived to be understood."

– Ralph Waldo Emerson

• • •

WHATEVER MAKES TEAM CLEAN WORK, MAKES LIFE WORK.

Team Clean	Life Lesson
Same night each week.	Learn to live with a schedule no matter how you are feeling that day or what else you have going on.
Working with others and dividing the work.	Learn to work as a member of a team.
Taking on the same jobs each week.	Taking ownership of a responsibility.

Work even when you are tired.	Learn to go to work on days even when you don't really feel like it.
Do someone's job for him when he is sick.	Learn to pitch in and help out even when it's not your assigned job.
Start Team Clean on time.	Learn to be prompt.
Work for a boss.	Learn to respect authority.
Learn to clean.	Learn an essential skill for when one lives on his or her own.
Pride in a job well done.	Learn that working hard has results.
Learn to work efficiently—paid by the job, not the hour.	Learn a good work ethic, not just to punch a clock.
Trading jobs, trading orderer rights.	Learn negotiating skills.
People are counting on you.	Learn that everyone's job matters.
Older grown children—setting up alternative night among themselves.	Learn to lead a group decision.
Can't skip Team Clean.	Learn not to call in sick.
Work off a "To Do" list or chart.	Learn to be organized and prepared.

*"Team Clean has taught me many things.
It has taught me responsibility and a
hard work ethic."*

-Kiersten

our daughter – started Team Clean at age 8

Checking In on Life After Team Clean

"And in the end, all will be well."

– Churchill

• • •

Team Clean has been such a gift to my marriage and to my family. It has created a glue that is pretty amazing. I feel like my husband is my partner in the house and in parenting.

Since the day Team Clean started, I have never felt like the house is my sole responsibility. I have never felt like the upkeep is all on me. I have never had to feel frustrated by a mess because "I have cleaned that up a million times!" I don't have to feel unappreciated for "all that I do to keep a clean house" because we all do it.

You might think that having a tradition like Team Clean would mean my house is perfect. That no matter when you stop by, you would always find it in complete order. Well, that is not true.

I was on my way to my son's lacrosse game one spring when my cell phone rang. He was calling in a panic. The team was on the bus and he had just realized he had the wrong game shorts with him. I knew if I turned around to get them, there was no way I would have them to him in time. I could picture his room at home; it was wall-to-wall clothes. His guitar was in the middle of his floor. His spare bike parts were probably on his bed. His school papers were most likely all over his dresser. There was no way to get to those needed lacrosse shorts without going into his room, and the only way to get them in time was to call on someone who was right near the house. I have a neighbor who had asked me many times how my house always looked so nice. I would always tell her it was because of Team Clean. Well, it was time to call that very neighbor. Her son was on the same team and I knew she would be passing my house about the right time. I dialed her number, and when she answered, I told her I was about to make her day. I said, "Dee, you know how you always ask me how my house is able to look so nice always?" She said, "Yes." I said, "Well, it's Wednesday, the day before Team Clean, and you are about to see the real thing. I need you to do me a favor." She agreed to the favor and went into my house. She got a true look at my son's room and I got a true gulp of pride swallowed. Bucky got his shorts in time and the team won.

Team Clean has taught me a few things along the way. One is that my house doesn't have to be perfect. I know it gets cleaned once a week. I know everything in our house has a place. I know we don't keep unnecessary things anymore. If the house isn't perfect at all times, it's okay.

I also am not too strict about the condition of my kids' rooms. They have to have the floor cleared for the vacuum once a week, and their clothes have to be put away on those days too. They have to get clothes to the laundry room if they want them washed by me. They have the option to wash their own clothes too. Two of them started doing most of their own wash in eighth grade while the other two still have me do it. Once a week, their trash cans get emptied, and every third week, their sheets get changed. I am okay with this.

It is so freeing to know there is more to life than a perfect house. I love to entertain and have people over. I love when my kids have their friends over. One of the most important things to me is to have friends visit often. Waiting for a perfect house would mean this doesn't happen.

• •

The first time I witnessed Team Clean, Carol's youngest was a mere five years old. You could barely see his head peeking from out of the whirlpool tub as he was diligently scrubbing away with a sponge bigger than he. I was shocked to be truthful! It looked like child labor to say the least. How could Carol possibly have him do such a "grown up" job? The funny thing was that the house seemed too put together with four kids and an assortment of friends scurrying in and out!

Fast forward to the present. That little kid is now a teenager (his siblings young adults). You couldn't find a more responsible, confident, and caring young man. The concept of Team Clean has taught invaluable lessons in teamwork, organization, and the importance of being a family unit. One day, a

young lady will thank her mother-in-law for the
brilliance of Team Clean!
-Silvia Hill
"Friend of Team Clean"

• •

"I do not picture it as cleaning my house or
vacuuming;
it is so much more than that.
It is mainly the combination of the entire thing."
-Bucky
our son – started Team Clean at age 10

• •

So, in the end, it really wasn't about a clean house. It turned out to be a way of raising our kids by building a weekly family tradition with them.
Team Clean became about instilling responsibility, dedication, respect, and a good work ethic, and creating a bond you would normally see between teammates (and even coaches with their players),all with a little Team Spirit!

Plus, it sure was nice having an assistant coach!

• •

Commenting on Your Comments

. . . .

"Champions know that success is inevitable; that there is no such thing as failure only feedback. They know that the best way to forecast the future is to create it."
– Michael J. Gelb

. . .

Over the years, I have taught other families the Team Clean system. As they have established the tradition in their homes, I have received great feedback. Following are some typical and frequently asked questions and my responses:

"Our family loves doing Team Clean. One of our kids always finishes earlier than everyone else and my husband gets so irritated that he is sitting around not doing anything while everyone else is working that he has him do extra stuff. It is stuff that needs to be done, but our son really hates it."

The life lesson here is that the kids are learning to take ownership of a job. That won't happen if Team Clean is just that they have to work for an hour. Everyone knows that people paid by the hour work slower and less efficiently than those paid by the job. Let your child be proud of taking ownership of his jobs, starting them on time and doing them well. He deserves to be done when he has completed them.

"We do Team Clean just like you have taught us except we have added the concept of "every others." We all have our normal jobs on the chart, but we also each have one job that is every other week. This process allows each of us to have one extra job since we rotate it every other week. It means being able to add items like cleaning out the inside of the fridge!"

We never added extra jobs because we felt it was important for kids to know what they were getting into and not feel like things were being piled on each week. Keeping the chart identical each week allows kids (and adults) to learn their jobs perfectly and become quite good at them. If your chart only changes every other week and then goes right back (meaning only two charts are in the rotation), I can see how family members could adjust to this schedule and how the household could benefit from the extra jobs! I like it.

"I read your book and love the concept! This past week, the kids had a day off from school and I gave everyone a Team Clean proj-

ect. It wasn't to the extent of what you do in the book, but it was a step in the right direction."

I am glad you like Team Clean! Be careful…giving everyone a job on his or her day off is not Team Clean. There is no reward/family activity here. Kids might think this is just a punishment. You had them do it together…so that makes it a team thing, but you need to incorporate the tradition part (activity/reward) and just as importantly establish a time they are aware of ahead of time.

"Wanted to let you know we are taking your Team Clean idea to the St. Vincent De Paul Society. Once a month, our family Team Clean is going to be cleaning their warehouse as a family."

What a great idea. Love that you are giving back! ☒

"Our oldest vacuums the rugs and he just vacuums the middle of all the rooms. He doesn't vacuum behind any furniture. I made him go back and move everything and get behind and under everything. I couldn't believe he thought he had finished vacuuming by just doing the middle…Kids!"

It is so much easier to teach the job correctly before it is done wrong than to go back and make a child redo it. Try your best to train the kids correctly for each job you give them. It is so disheartening for a child to hear he has done it wrong or has to redo a job. Often, I overlook a sloppy job and just make it a point to show the child the correct way the next week before we start. It is very rare that I would have someone go back and redo a sloppy job. My husband disagrees with this…but I try to treat the kids the way I would want to be treated after cleaning for forty-five minutes. I know the last thing I would want to hear is what I did wrong! (Think about how it feels when you have done something great and someone walks in and notices the *one* mistake or the *one* thing you haven't done yet…not a good feeling.)

"We do Team Clean on different days each week. Sometimes we do the food part first if we start Team Clean late on a weekend day and we just make the meal lunch. It seems like the kids want to do this Team Clean thing, but we can't really get on track."

In terms of picking a day, I can't stress enough how important it is to pick a regular day and time. Imagine someone waking you up one day and saying, "I have decided you have to get dressed up in a suit and be at work in thirty minutes," and then the next week walking in on a Friday evening and saying, "Put on a suit; you need to be at work in a half hour." It would be really tough to change gears and mentally accept that you have to go along with the plan each time. In life, you might never find the best workday or time, but knowing it ahead of time really helps you accept and prepare for it. This is true for Team Clean also.

In terms of eating before you clean, that's like having happy hour and chilling before work! It would be really hard to go to work after that second margarita! For a kid, it's almost like getting the paycheck, spending it on what he or she wanted to buy, enjoying the item, and *then* going to work to work it off!

"We can't seem to find a night that works. We are thinking of trying a Saturday or Sunday morning and then ordering lunch. What do you think?"

I think this is fine. As long as you establish your day and time and your tradition afterwards, it should work. Try the best you can to look into the future and think of all the stages your family has left and what might work best for the long term. Teenagers are not too happy about waking up early or being kept home on a weekend night.

"We barely get through our evenings now; how did you ever fit in Team Clean?

Remember that the hour and a half to two hours your entire Team Clean will take (this includes the reward) really just replaces dinner prep and cleanup time. Don't tell the kids, but you were working anyway; now you just have help!

"I want to start Team Clean right now! My kids seem too young. They are two and seven. Can I do it?"

You sure can! The key is to start a family night. You can rush through cleaning a whole house pretty fast even when just three "able" people are part of the process. Make sure to include the two year old though. He/she can move things where you need them to go. Like put the dustpan or dirty rags away. Seven year olds can vacuum and clean a toilet if you teach them. The teaching days are the most important ones. You might not even be able to do your own jobs the first time or two, but that's okay. You will be glad you trained the kids correctly. Show your pride in their jobs when they are done. They should have to come get you, "the inspector," to sign off on their jobs when they are complete. Maybe even let them hear you call Grandma and brag about what they did!

Remember this: Whatever you get done on Team Clean night is more than you were doing before, and you are starting a habit and tradition. The younger your kids are, the better. They won't remember a time before Team Clean and will accept it as a part of life. If you have to "supplement" (hire help, clean in secret on your own, etc.) when your kids are young, then do it, but believe me, it won't be long before you are only cleaning once a week, and it won't be alone!

"My husband says he thinks Team Clean is a good idea, but he just won't adhere to a weekly schedule. It is all up to me. How do I make this happen if he won't lead it?"

Communication is the key. You need to tell him separately from the night of Team Clean that this is important to you and that you want to try it. You should tell him that Team Clean will mean less nagging from you for household help in the end. Team Clean will give him his weekends. Tell him you understand that he is tired and that he is not excited about doing a household chore, but if everyone just sucks it up and does one little part, it makes life easier for everyone. His involvement will mean the kids will cooperate, and you need that from him. The fun family time will be worth it in the end. We have found that making Team Clean be on Thursday has put a change in the routine of the "same old, same old" of the week night schedule and allowed us to feel like we are starting the weekend a little early.

And lastly…does he get a headache every week when Team Clean is about to start? Maybe tell him you promise never to get a headache on Team Clean Night! (Remember…weekly rewards! ☒

Want more interaction?

Join us on Facebook! www.facebook.com/TheTeamClean

Follow us on Twitter www.twitter.com/TheTeamClean

Ask Carol Paul questions and get answers

carol@TheTeamClean.com

Visit us at www.TheTeamClean.com

Prepping for the Weekly Team Clean

● ●

"By failing to prepare, you are preparing to fail."
– Benjamin Franklin

● ● ●

Coaches prep for games by making game plans. Often they review game films and talk about past successes and mistakes. They talk about future substitutions, new equipment, new plays, etc. They always get feedback from their other coach. Nobody just shows up on game day unprepared. The same holds true for Team Clean.

If you establish Team Clean correctly in your house, you will find that you will only be cleaning your house once a week, and that it will never be alone. Everyone who lives in your household will always be part of your cleaning crew. However, there are a few extra steps that Team Clean needs from you. I have broken them into five parts. The first three are ones that you will have to concentrate on in the beginning stages of your Team Clean, but over time, you will no longer need to do them. The final two, I still do to this day!

START-UP NEEDS:

I. NOTES

Go back through this book and highlight all the areas you think are important to your family's Team Clean. Maybe a section really focused on the ages of your family, or maybe I talked about a difficulty you see in one of your children or your household. Highlight anything you think might be a good reference when it comes time to troubleshooting or personalizing your Team Clean.

Add notes to the "take note" section at the end of this book. Now is the time to write all of this down. If anything comes to mind that you think might be good for your family's new tradition, jot it down. If you note it now, you are more apt to follow the advice as you establish your family's Team Clean. You are about to start a project, and the more plans and notes you make, the better.

II. REVIEW

For thirteen years, I ran our children's school's annual family FUNDAY. I loved every minute of it. I was blessed to work with the most amazing, positive, energetic, and creative people. Spending time with them brought such joy to me! The FUNDAY committee members bonded through our weekly planning meetings. (Like most teams do!) We found that brainstorming, prepping, taking notes, listening to each other's ideas, etc. made FUNDAY a great event. But I have to say that three key elements probably can be attributed to what truly took it a notch above other school carnivals: finding the truly best person for each chair position, sharing the work among many hands, and taking the wrap-up meeting after the event seriously. These were the keys to the FUNDAY's success.

The very premise of Team Clean already covers one of the three keys, and that's sharing the work. It is your job as leader to make sure people are in the right positions, and that covers key two. So here I will talk about the last of the three success keys: the wrap-up meeting. I highly suggest you have your own little wrap-up meeting with yourself (or maybe with your spouse) after your first few Team Cleans. Jot things down like you would in a diary. Note what goes well, and what doesn't go well. Write down ideas you have. Brainstorm as much as you can.

I suggest you combine the notes you take while reading this book (including all the highlighted ones) and the review notes you take after your initial Team Cleans and put them all together in the "take note" section at the end of this book.

III. CRAM FOR THE EXAM!

Each week, re-read your full "take notes" section the day before Team Clean as your pre-game "pep talk." Use it to help alter your chart and perfect it. You will start to see your Team Clean get better and better each week. It will slowly become a custom-built Team Clean perfect for your family!

ONGOING NEEDS:

BUY

Outside of Team Clean night, I make sure we always have everything we need for Team Clean. To ease this chore, I buy in bulk when we are out of items. In fact, in the Fall of 2011, I got hooked on TheKrazyCouponLady and now my supply is never-ending!

PREP

Each Thursday morning, after the last shower is taken, I quickly prep for Team Clean. The seven steps below take me fifteen minutes total and that includes starting the washing machine. There is no reason to drag it out. I follow my dad's philosophy here: "Be quick, but don't hurry!"

- Grab dirty dish towels and rags and get to laundry

- Grab all dirty towels (including hand towels) and start a load of wash

- Remove all bath rugs

- Put the washable ones in the wash

- Place the ones that can be vacuumed on rugs nearest bathroom (for the rug vac person to vacuum them before replacing)

- Strip our bed and one kid's bed and put sheets in laundry room

- Quickly run through the house and grab everyone's personal items and put them in "their spot" or in their bedroom

- If there are clean clothes piles to go to bedrooms…get them there

- Clear all surfaces like I would for a cleaning service…are there dishes or items on tables that need to be put in the kitchen?

…and now the house is ready for my cleaning crew to come!

Laying the Foundation for Team Clean

● ●

"I'll huff and I'll puff and I'll blow your house in."
– The Big Bad Wolf

● ● ●

When it was time for The Three Little Pigs to leave home and seek their fortunes, they all chose to go about it slightly differently. The first pig chose the quickest way, the second pig chose a way that was just better than the first pig's, and the third pig chose the way with the strongest foundation. Some of the smaller decisions they might have made, like paint colors for the walls or what's for dinner, wouldn't have affected the outcome they had with the Big Bad Wolf, but the main building materials they chose for their homes were important to their fates. We all know who fared the best!

So are you ready to start the fortune of Team Clean for your family? Like building a cardhouse or playing Jenga, the beginning steps and moves you make matter more than anything else. The smaller touches you add to make your Team Clean fit your personal family will be like choosing your wall paint colors or putting the top card on your cardhouse, but for now, build your foundation strong. Know that these base Team Clean materials are key.

My family has been doing Team Clean religiously for over twelve years, spanning many ages, moods, good and bad childhood stages, and I have had the fun of witnessing other families try my system too. Let me share what I have learned to be the key foundation materials of Team Clean. I think they hold true no matter what family situation you are in (two parents, single parent, younger kids, older kids, unrelated family members, multiple generations, lots of kids and/or only children).

The foundation materials might seem like little things, but they matter. There is a reason for them. I include them because they are the key ingredients that teach the life lessons your children will take from this experience. They can be the hinge on whether your Team Clean works or not. Using the materials can be the difference between a long-term successful Team Clean family tradition and a family cleaning time that fizzles out within a few months.

TEAM CLEAN'S FOUNDATION MATERIALS

- Team Clean has two parts—it is more than a weekly cleaning ritual—it's a family tradition! (Do not skip the second part.)

- The reward part of Team Clean should include a meal, which you do not prep during Team Clean, and a simple activity—these should stay the same each week; that's the only way to form a tradition.

- Keep Team Clean the same night each week.

- Keep Team Clean the same time frame each week.

- Keep jobs the same each week.

- Everyone who lives in your house must be part of the team.

- Use the chart every week.

- Don't ever skip Team Clean.

- Take the time to teach the job right the first time—it's hard to correct a bad habit.

- Every team needs a good coach—show up and coach every week!

- Keep up with your quarterly cleans.

TEAM CLEAN

Same Meal & Activity

Don't Skip Part II	Same Night

Everyone Participates

Same Time	Same Jobs

Use The Chart

No Skipping	Show Up & Coach

Quarterly Cleans

Teach The Jobs Well

A Final Note

• •

"To get something you never had,
you have to do something you never did."
– Anonymous

• • •

Now that you have read *Team Clean*, what next? You can read all the diet books you want, but until you apply the wisdom, you won't lose weight. My friend often jokes, "I have looked at my treadmill every day for the last two weeks, and I still I haven't lost a pound! That dumb salesman swore it would work!" The same holds true here. You now have the knowledge of how to bring Team Clean to your family. You know its benefits. Are you ready to start?

I challenge you to commit to trying the Team Clean system for ninety days. Get out a marker and put an "X" on the calendar for three months from today. Show your family members that they are the most important people in your life. In the end, they will be the people you spend more time with in your life than anyone else you know. Take the time now to build a relationship with them.

I encourage you to create your personal family Team Clean by deciding on ten actions. What are your top ten actions going to be? Look back through the chapters. Look through the notes you took while reading. Come up with your list of the ten most important things you plan to do to get your team going.

In this book, you have learned how to declutter your house, how to establish a weekly cleaning ritual that your entire family will participate in, and how to go beyond cleaning to create a family bonding time your children will look forward to. So many books say to go at it alone or they teach you tricks or work-arounds for cleaning or organizing. This one has shown you how to spend *less* time cleaning and has taught you a way never to do it alone again. It has the added bonus of enriching your kids' lives—talk about a de-stressor all around! Just imagine some of the awful teenage and future years you can avoid!

I encourage you to contact me by email: carol@theteamclean. com. I would love to help you with YOUR Team Clean in any way I can!

Okay. Now bring it in…bring it in…huddle up.

I wish you good luck.
I know you will succeed and have less stress in your life.
Now go out there and reclaim your home and
re-strengthen your family.

One…Two…Three…Team Clean!

Let's win this!

Carol Paul

TAKE NOTE...

TAKE NOTE...

_____
_____
_____
_____
_____
_____
_____
_____
_____
_____
_____
_____
_____
_____
_____
_____
_____
_____
_____
_____
_____
_____
_____
_____
_____
_____
_____
_____
_____
_____

TAKE NOTE...

TAKE NOTE...

TAKE NOTE...

APPENDIX I:
Chart Samples

●●●●●●●●●●●●●●●●●●●●●●●●●●●●●●●●●●●●

Team Clean: _____

Jobs					
Alexa (8 yr old)	Vacuum All Rugs	Trash	Replace Toilet Paper/Refill Soap	Bedroom	
Reese (6 yr old)	Vacuum All Bathroom Floors	Vacuum Kitchen Floors	Vacuum All Hard Floors	Bedroom	
Jackson (3 yr old)	Kitchen Chairs	Dust/Wipe Steps	Pick-Up Toys	Bathroom Floors	
Terri (Mom)	1/2 Bath	1/2 Bath	Full Bath	Full Bath	Sheets, Towels, Rugs
Joe (Dad)	Stove & Micro-wave	Counters	Sink	Fridge	Kitchen Table

Team Clean: _____

Jobs

Nick (14 yr old)	Master bath Shower	Master Bath Tub	Master Bath Toilet	Master Bath Sinks & Mirrors	Bedroom
Brian (11 yr old)	Kids Bath, Sink & Mirror	Kids Bath Toilet	Guest Bath Sink & Mirror	Guest Bath Toilet	Bedroom
Greg (9 yr old)	Vacuum All Bathroom Floors	Vacuum Kitchen Floor	Vacuum Foyer	All Trash	Bedroom
Kevin (6 yr old)	Replace Toilet Paper	News-papers	Kitchen Table	Kitchen Chairs	Bderoom
Caitlin (4 yr old)	Master Bath Floor	Wipe Steps	Kids Bath Floor	Guest Bath Floor	Bedroom
Cathy (Mom)	Stove & Micro-wave	Counters	Sink	Fridge	Sheets, Towels & Rugs
Mike (Dad)	Vaccum All Rugs	Vacuum Basement Steps	Vacuum Square Landing Rug		

Team Clean: _____

Jobs

Lauren (12 yr old)	Vacuum All Rugs	2nd Floor Trash	Bedroom		
Peter (8 yr old)	Vacuum Kitchen Floors	Vacuum Bathroom Floors	Vacuum All Hard Floors	1st Floor Trash	Bedroom
Sarah (6 yr old)	Clean Bathroom & Laundry Room Floors	Change Kitty Litter	Replace Toilet Paper, Refill Soap	Bedroom	
Barb (Mom)	Bathroom 1	Bathroom 2	Bathroom 3	Sheets, Towels & Rugs	
Pete (Dad)	Stove & Micro-wave	Counters	Sink	Fridge	Kitchen Table

Team Clean: _____

Jobs

William (14 yr old)	Vacuum All Rugs	Trash	Bedroom		
Charlie (12 yr old)	Vacuum Kitchen Floors	Vacuum Bathroom Floors	Vacuum All Hard Floors	Sweep Front Porch	Bedroom
Joey (10 yr old)	Clean Bathroom & Laundry Room Floors	Clean Tubs & Showers	Replace Toilet Paper, Refill Soap	Bedroom	
Betsy (Mom)	Bathroom 1	Bathroom 2	Bathroom 3	Bathroom 4	Sheets, Towels & Rugs
Kevin (Dad)	Stove & Micro-wave	Counters	Sink	Fridge	Kitchen Table

Team Clean: _____

Jobs

Megan (10 yr old)	Vacuum All Rugs	Vacuum Basement Steps	Clean Bathroom Floors	Bedroom	
Micky (8 yr old)	Vacuum All Bathroom Floors	Vacuum Kitchen Floors	Vacuum Foyer	All Trash	Bedroom
Elizabeth (Mom)	Bath 1	Bath 2	Bathroom 3	Refill Toilet Paper & Refill Soaps	Sheets, Towels & Rugs
Brendan (Dad)	Stove & Micro-wave	Counters	Sink	Fridge	Kitchen Table

Team Clean: _____

Kristin (18 yr old)	Vacuum Rugs	Vacuum Steps	Bedroom		
Katie (16 yr old)	Vacuum Middle Level Wood Floor	Vacuum Basement Floor & Hall	Vacuum Bathroom & Laundry Floors	Bedroom	
Collen (14 yr old)	Clean Laundry Room Floor	Clean Bath & Laundry Floors	Trash & Recycling	Bedroom	
Annie (Mom)	Kids Bath	Master Bath	1/2 Bath	1/2 Bath	Sheets, Towels & Rugs
Paul (Dad)	Kitchen Table, Micro-wave, Stove	Toaster Oven, Can Opener, Clean/ Shine Sink	Water Plants, Dust, Change Light Bulbs	Bleach Counters	

Team Clean: _____

Ashley (7 yr old)	Vacuum All Rugs	Trash	Refill Toilet Paper	Refill Soap	Bedroom
Tyler (4 yr old)	Vacuum All Bathroom Floors	Vacuum Kitchen Floor	Clean Bathroom Floors	Clean Kitchen Chairs	Bedroom
Melissa (Mom)	Bath 1	Bath 2	Bath 3	Sheets, Towels & Rugs	
Fred (Dad)	Stove & Micro-wave	Counters	Sink	Fridge	Kitchen Table

Team Clean: _____

Alex (10 yr old)	Bathroom Sink, Toilet Mirror, Floor	Bathroom Sink, Toilet Mirror, Shower, Floor	Bedroom		
Emma (8 yr old)	Vacuum All Rugs	Vacuum All Hard Floors Including Bathrooms -Do Bathrooms First!	Bedroom		
Bridget (Mom)	Stove & Micro-wave	Counters	Sink & Kitchen Table	Trash	Towels, Sheets 7 Rugs

APPENDIX II:
Job Samples

JOBS A TWO YEAR OLD CAN DO

- Tidy-up bedroom (loosely define!)

- Put toys away

- Put magazines in the recycling spot

- Dust

- Wipe table with wet rag

- Dust windowsills

- Carry dirty towels to laundry room

- Bring "items needed" to family members who are cleaning

JOBS A THREE YEAR OLD CAN DO

- Tidy-up bedroom
- Put toys away in correct location
- Dust
- Wipe appropriate surfaces with damp rag
- Hold dustpan
- Put clean rags back to where you keep them
- Carry dirty towels to laundry room
- Carry tied up wastebasket bags outside
- Carry new toilet paper rolls to bathrooms

JOBS A FOUR YEAR OLD CAN DO

- Tidy-up bedroom

- Help make beds (puts pillows on)

- Vacuum with a shop vacuum

- Put folded clothes away

- Help empty trash cans—tie bags

- Feed pets

- Sort clothes by colors, darks, whites

- Dust hardwood steps

- Wipe surfaces

- Clean doorknobs

JOBS A FIVE YEAR OLD CAN DO

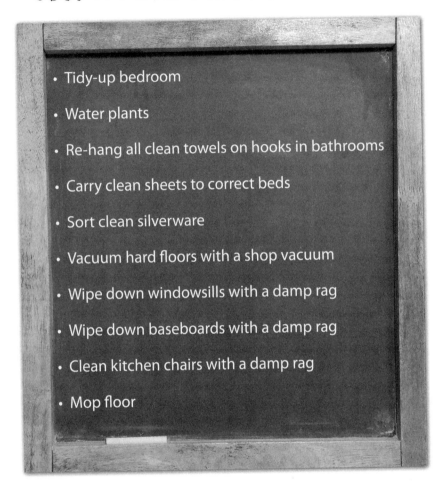

- Tidy-up bedroom

- Water plants

- Re-hang all clean towels on hooks in bathrooms

- Carry clean sheets to correct beds

- Sort clean silverware

- Vacuum hard floors with a shop vacuum

- Wipe down windowsills with a damp rag

- Wipe down baseboards with a damp rag

- Clean kitchen chairs with a damp rag

- Mop floor

JOBS A SIX YEAR OLD CAN DO

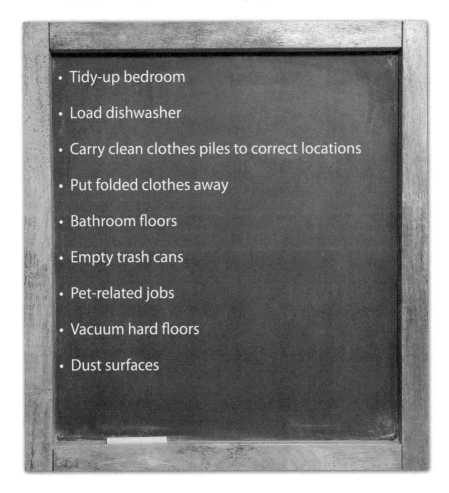

- Tidy-up bedroom

- Load dishwasher

- Carry clean clothes piles to correct locations

- Put folded clothes away

- Bathroom floors

- Empty trash cans

- Pet-related jobs

- Vacuum hard floors

- Dust surfaces

JOBS A SEVEN YEAR OLD CAN DO

- Tidy-up bedroom
- Sweep front porch
- Clean showers
- Clean bathtubs
- Change lightbulbs
- Fold clothes
- Clean & buff kitchen table
- Start the wash (towels, sheets)
- Vacuum floors

JOBS AN EIGHT YEAR OLD CAN DO

- Tidy-up bedroom
- Clean toilets
- Clean bathroom sinks
- Clean mirrors
- Vacuum rugs
- Spray and wipe kitchen counters
- Disinfect the kitchen sink
- Refill hand soaps
- Vacuum floors
- Empty trash

About the Author

• •

Carol Paul is the author of *Team Clean* which was published in the Summer of 2013. She is a professional speaker, Team Clean coach, and co-owner of a basketball camp. She lives with her husband Steve (of over twenty-six years) and her four children in Bowie, Maryland. She and her husband established Team Clean in their family home in the Fall of 2000. Since 1991, she has co-owned a basketball camp with her father and brother. She spends her summers, with her family, in Frostburg, Maryland, where the camps have been located since 1998. Each season, they instruct 2,500 boys and girls and over 300 coaches from all over the world. On the side, she manages a couple of beach house rentals and loves to help at the EPIC Brands' Reach-the-Beach Cheer events (her sister's company). She has chaired several community non-profit events over the years, including St. Pius X FUNDAY, Ascension OKTOBERFEST, and The Chorbajian Children's Fundraiser. She serves on numerous committees including two annual events: The St. Ambrose Spaghetti Dinner and The St. Ambrose Golf Tournament. She formed and coached a school dance team for her local elementary school in 2002. She started the ACT youth group in 2007 and built it around four cornerstones: faith, fundraising, free-aid to the needy, and fun. She served quite a few years for her local school's

Home and School Association and the school board. She often shares her belief that to be happy, you should live by four Ps: marry the right person (and be the right person to be married to), make and keep priorities, be positive—always, and play (have fun). She truly enjoys running events, but her main passion is her family. (And spending time at the beach!)

I Can Coach You on How to Coach Your Team!

· ·

My help doesn't stop with this book. I can be there for you and your family as much as you need me. Do you have questions that weren't answered in this book? Do you need help making your chart? Do you want to set up time to go over your plan?

Check out below all that *Team Clean* has to offer you!

www.TheTeamClean.com

- Get the latest about what is going on with us at *Team Clean*

- Ask Carol Paul questions and get answers!

- Download a Team Clean chart for your family

- Schedule Carol Paul to speak at your next event (no matter how big or small!)

- Get new Team Clean Building Blocks as they come out!

Become our friend on Facebook!
www.facebook.com/TheTeamClean

- Interact with other families who are establishing Team Clean in their homes

- Share your success stories

- Read about other families' successes (and bloopers!)

- Post questions and get answers

Follow us on Twitter! www.twitter.com/TheTeamClean

- Get the latest about what is going on with us at *Team Clean*

- Get Team Clean Building Blocks sent to your Twitter account!

- Be the first to learn about special offers you can win!

Contact:

Carol@TheTeamClean.com

Team Clean

5009 Patuxent Riding Lane

Bowie, MD 20715

www.TheTeamClean.com

Carol Paul will come speak to your group...

• •

Are you a member of a club, group, or organization? You can have Carol Paul come out to speak to you! No club is too big or small. She is enthusiastic and loves to share her message! Let her energize your:

- Book Club
- Church Group
- Retreat
- Family
- Parent Teacher Association (PTA)

- Moms' Group
- Play Group
- School Group
- Neighborhood
- You name it!

Contact:

Carol@TheTeamClean.com

Team Clean

5009 Patuxent Riding Lane

Bowie, MD 20715

www.TheTeamClean.com

Coach Wootten's Basketball Camp

● ●

Teaching Fundamentals & Values to young men & women Since 1961

● ● ●

Carol Paul co-owns Coach Wootten's Basketball Camp with her father, Morgan Wootten, and her brother, Joe Wootten. She has been part of the operations since 1991.

Currently, the camps are located in Frostburg, Maryland. They are the oldest basketball camps in the world. They are true teaching camps for the game of basketball and they serve boys and girls ages nine to eighteen. Coach Wootten does all the teaching of the fundamentals himself and still sleeps in the dorms and eats in the dining hall. The camps are known for tight supervision and non-stop enthusiasm.

The camps' goal is to take each camper and develop him or her into a well-rounded, complete basketball player. The philosophy is to instill the fundamentals of the game along with a proper attitude toward it. Confidence, teamwork, effort, and sportsmanship are all stressed. The coaches constantly remind their campers that these values are not only important on the court but also in family, school, and life.

Each summer, they instruct more than 3,000 athletes and over 400 coaches from all over the world. They work with beginners all the way to the high school star.

www.CoachWootten.com